Historical American Biographies

JOHN PAUL JONES

Father of the American Navy

Alison Davis Tibbitts

Enslow Publishers, Inc.

40 Industrial Road   PO Box 38
Box 398   Aldershot
Berkeley Heights, NJ 07922   Hants GU12 6BP
USA   UK

http://www.enslow.com

Dedication

For my Dad, Rear Admiral James Robert Davis, United States Naval Academy, Class of 1934. He was a great admirer of John Paul Jones.

Copyright © 2002 by Alison Davis Tibbitts

Library of Congress Cataloging-in-Publication Data

Tibbitts, Alison.
    John Paul Jones : father of the American navy / Alison Tibbitts.
      p. cm. — (Historical American biographies)
    Includes bibliographical references and index.
    ISBN 0-7660-1448-7
    1. Jones, John Paul, 1747–1792—Juvenile literature. 2. Admirals—United States—Biography—Juvenile literature. 3. United States. Navy—Biography—Juvenile literature. 4. United States—History—Revolution, 1775–1783—Naval operations—Juvenile literature. [1. Jones, John Paul, 1747–1792. 2. Admirals. 3. United States. Navy—Biography. 4. United States—History—Revolution, 1775–1783.] I. Title. II. Series.
    E207 .J7 T56   2002
    973.3'5'092
                           2001000703

Printed in the United States of America

10 9 8 7 6 5 4 3 2 1

Illustration Credits: Courtesy John G. Brodie, pp. 4, 11, 22, 42, 49, 55, 63, 69, 99; Enslow Publishers, Inc., pp. 8, 61, 84; Bob Grieser/ATL, pp. 100, 114, 116; National Archives and Records Administration, pp. 28, 30, 33, 70, 75, 81, 87, 104; Courtesy U.S. Naval Academy Museum, pp. 38, 54, 82, 93, 105.

Cover Illustration: Portrait of John Paul Jones, Courtesy of U.S. Navel Academy Museum. Background: National Archives and Records Administration.

CONTENTS

This portrait of John Paul Jones was painted by famed American artist Charles Willson Peale. It hangs today at Independence Hall in Philadelphia, Pennsylvania.

THE SUMMER CRUISE

America declared its independence from Great Britain in 1776. Within two years, the new nation had allied with France to fight against the British. In August and September 1779, Captain John Paul Jones of the United States Navy cruised the British Isles aboard his flagship, *Bonhomme Richard*.

Jones was the commodore, or senior captain, in command of a five-vessel squadron. In addition to the *Bonhomme Richard*, his group included America's *Alliance* and France's *Pallas*, *Vengeance*, and *Cerf*. Jones expected his ships to work as a team. That sometimes proved difficult when a captain sailed off for a time to pursue his own interests.

Jones's orders for the six-week cruise did not mention specific destinations. He planned to be an

unpredictable nuisance, turning up without warning to disrupt, distract, and destroy British ships. While Jones diverted British naval resources in the west, Spain and France planned to invade England from the southeast.

Jones's squadron began a brief trip on June 17, 1779, to test the ships' equipment. On the second night out, a collision occurred between *Alliance* and *Richard* that broke the latter's bowsprit. It was repaired when the squadron returned to port in Lorient, France, to load supplies for the longer cruise. The squadron departed again on August 14. Jones set a course along the west coast of Ireland, through the Orkney Islands north of Scotland, across the North Sea, and south along the east coast of Scotland and England to Holland.

An important mission of every cruise was to capture British ships, called "prizes." These were sold in friendly ports to buyers who could pay cash. Officers and crewmen shared the profits. *Bonhomme Richard* carried more than two hundred prisoners below deck as it neared England's east coast. They came from vessels the squadron had captured, burned, or sunk during the voyage. They would eventually be exchanged for imprisoned Americans.

On September 22, Jones raised Great Britain's flag, the Union Jack, and another flag, signaling to harbor pilots ashore that *Richard* needed assistance. Jones wanted to navigate the shallow channel into the Humber River and capture a merchant convoy. Two pilots saw the Union Jack, assumed *Richard* was British, and responded to Jones's signal. When they

Signal Flags

Sailing ships carried flags for communication and recognition. A flag atop the mast, visible from a distance, indicated a ship's origin. The commanding officer's flag identified a battle group's flagship, or central command post. A flagship combined varied flags to send specific messages to other ships, telling them to change direction, giving information on battle conditions, danger, surrender, and many other necessary details.

came aboard, Jones asked them for local shipping news.

One pilot reported that a large fleet of merchant ships was due from the Baltic Sea any day. Escorted by British warships H.M.S. *Serapis* and H.M.S. *Countess of Scarborough*, the fleet carried timber and a valuable cargo of heavy fabric for winter uniforms. Jones knew that American General George Washington's troops in New York urgently needed such cloth. He dismissed the pilots.

Pallas, *Alliance*, *Bonhomme Richard*, and *Vengeance* cruised England's coastline through the morning of September 23. The squadron lingered near Flamborough Head, a prominent landmark overlooking the North Sea. The dangerous shoreline along the base of chalky cliffs had hidden reefs, powerful currents, and almost no beach.

In the early afternoon, Jones ordered his crew to prepare for action. The men liked their captain and

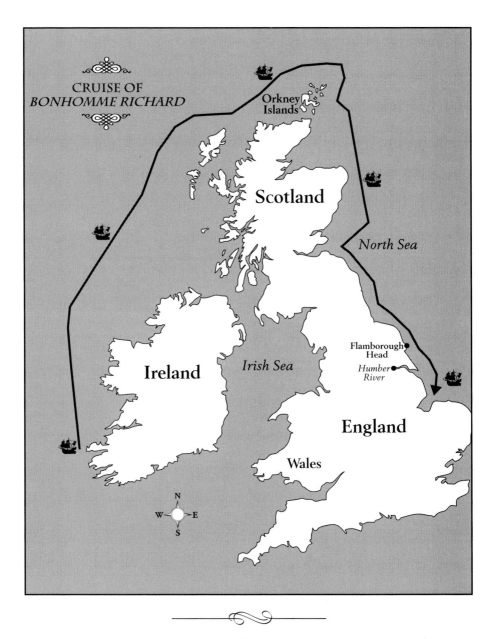

CRUISE OF
BONHOMME RICHARD

Orkney
Islands

Scotland

North Sea

Ireland

Irish Sea

Flamborough
Head

*Humber
River*

England

Wales

N
W • E
S

This map shows the route taken by the Bonhomme Richard *around
the British Isles in August and September 1779.*

were loyal to him, which was not the case on every ship, or for every captain. Jones was a demanding, quick-tempered man who did not tolerate excuses or carelessness. He expected top performance from his crew because he knew everyone's safety depended on it.

In mid-afternoon, Jones scanned the horizon for perhaps the hundredth time. At last, he saw a distant cluster of sails, indicating the arrival of forty-one merchant ships. From miles away, he recognized the type of vessel Great Britain used to transport supplies. Two warships guarded the slow-moving fleet as it came toward Jones.

Captain Richard Pearson of Britain's Royal Navy vessel *Serapis* knew what to expect. Having been warned of foreign ships in the region, he was not surprised to find them. Sailors atop the mast spotted *Richard* around noon. Everyone on deck could see it by four o'clock.

Serapis and *Countess of Scarborough* stationed themselves between the Americans and the merchant ships. Pearson signaled them to hug the shoreline, fire guns, and flap some sails as they hastened to safety under the guns of Scarborough Castle. These distress signals would alert British citizens on shore to potential danger.

Serapis and *Countess of Scarborough* maintained their positions. Pearson knew his frigate was the superior battle craft. *Serapis* was quick and responsive, partly because it had a smooth copper bottom. Its two decks held forty-four new cannons. The *Countess*

of Scarborough carried twenty more. Pearson controlled enormous firepower.

Aboard *Bonhomme Richard*, Captain Jones realized that the fight would not be evenly matched. He had supervised *Richard*'s conversion from merchant ship to warship months earlier. He knew its limitations. The thirteen-year-old vessel had made many cargo voyages to China and India in its day. *Richard* was reliable, but it was slow and not very agile. It had some rotting timbers and it leaked occasionally. Many of its forty guns were unpredictable, if they worked at all.

With light winds and ten miles of open ocean, the enemies took around three hours to approach each other. Jones knew he had to defeat *Serapis* and *Countess of Scarborough* before he could even consider attacking the merchant fleet. He moved to the helm and began issuing orders.

Shortly before sunset, *Richard*'s crew manned their battle stations. Midshipman Nathaniel Fanning sent fourteen French Marine sharpshooters up to a platform forty feet above the deck for a clear view of the enemy below. Twenty-four men scrambled up *Richard*'s masts into the network of ropes called riggings. Dr. Lawrence Brooke laid out cloths and canvas to receive the wounded. He set out jugs of rum and ale to numb their pain.

At dusk, Jones signaled his squadron to form a line of battle. Although he was in command, the captains of the other ships in his squadron ignored him. *Alliance* left the scene. *Vengeance* glided around in circles. *Pallas* dropped behind the battle line, but returned

Captain Jones directed his men in the midst of battle between Bonhomme Richard *and H.M.S.* Serapis *on September 23, 1779.*

later to attack *Countess of Scarborough*. *Richard* was left to fight alone.

In early evening, guns were loaded. Crewmen held lighted matches and flints over the cannons' touch-holes, prepared to fire. *Richard* approached *Serapis*'s port, or left, side. Marines aloft selected their targets. Voices grew silent. Bright moonlight reflected off the water. *Richard*'s Midshipman Fanning described the scene as "a clear cool evening with practically no wind and the sea as smooth as glass."[1]

At twenty minutes past seven o'clock, *Serapis* approached *Richard*, coming within a hundred yards. Captain Pearson called for identification. With the British flag flying from *Richard*'s mast, Jones ordered his helmsman, Samuel Stacey, to answer, "The Royal Princess."[2]

"Repeat the name, or I will fire into you," Pearson shouted.[3] Jones ordered his crew to haul down the Union Jack and hoist America's Stars and Stripes. He signaled to the men on *Richard*'s starboard, or right, side to begin firing as *Serapis* let go its first shots. The most important naval battle of the American Revolution had begun.

2

GOING TO SEA

John Paul was born on July 6, 1747. He was named after his father. Jones was not part of the family name. The Pauls lived in a three-room stone house at Arbigland, an estate in Kirkbean Parish, Kirkcudbrightshire, Scotland. The house had been a wedding present from the estate's owner, William Craik. John Paul, Sr., was a talented gardener. His wife, Jean, had been Craik's housekeeper.

Arbigland was a beautiful estate near the shore. Wildflowers grew all year and rich soil produced plentiful vegetables and grains. Sheep and cows grazed in fields separated by low stone walls. The scent of sea air came from the nearby Firth of Solway, a river separating England and Scotland. Fishermen filled their

nets in the firth as they watched passing ships from around the world.

The Pauls had seven children, two of whom died in infancy. William was nine when his brother, John, Jr., arrived. John's older sisters were Elizabeth, who never married, and Janet Taylor, who married a shopkeeper. Mary Ann, the youngest, married a British seaman. When he died, she married a shopkeeper named Lowden.

Many families around Arbigland were Presbyterians who belonged to the Church of Scotland. They attended Sunday services at their church in Kirkbean Parish. From the age of seven, John and his friends walked a mile each way to the church school. They wore the sturdy homespun wool clothes handed down from son to son.

Reverend James Hogg was their parson and school-master. He taught his students well. John could read, write, and speak some French and Latin by the age of thirteen when he left school to support himself. He was sandy-haired, a bit below average height, with hazel eyes and big ideas about his future. Because he considered William Craik a perfect gentleman, John intended to work his way up in society and have respectable friends like Craik.

John knew farming was not for him. He heard the call of the sea throughout his boyhood. As a child, he played almost daily in a creek near the Solway, direct-ing his friends' boats in mock battles. Later, with his parents' permission, he walked often to the small port of Carsethorn, a mile and a half from Arbigland. He explored the boats, talked with sailors and fishermen, and asked about life at sea.

John knew his family had no special connections to help him find work in a big city, or secure a midshipman's appointment to begin a career in Great Britain's Royal Navy. Some boys asked their ministers to arrange university scholarships. They became doctors, teachers, or ministers, as had Reverend Hogg. John decided his best choice was to join the British merchant marine. These cargo ships carried imported and exported goods all over the world.

Early Days at Sea

The Pauls' neighbor knew a merchant and shipowner named John Younger at the port across the Solway in Whitehaven, England. Younger needed an apprentice seaman on a vessel leaving for the West Indies and Virginia. John's parents approved, so he packed a sea chest and sailed to Whitehaven to seek the job.

Early in 1761, John signed an agreement with Younger to work as an apprentice for seven years. He would learn expert seamanship, have a place to live, and receive a small wage each time the ship returned to Whitehaven. His first job was as a ship's boy. He was assigned to do menial tasks for Captain Robert Benson aboard *Friendship*.

John worked long, exhausting days. He and the crew slept in hammocks suspended from overhead beams in the bow of the ship below the deck. As the newest crew member, his hammock was in the most

Life Aboard Ship

Life on sailing ships has been described as "being jailed, with the added risk of drowning."[1] There was bad food, poor ventilation, and diseases such as malaria and cholera. Discipline for misbehavior was swift. One severe punishment was flogging with a leather whip. Another was keelhauling, where the rule breaker was dragged by a rope from one side of the ship to the other, underwater. Not everyone survived the ordeal.

cramped place. He fell asleep as the hammock swayed gently, or roughly, depending on the waves rocking the boat.

Friendship arrived at the island Barbados in the West Indies on May 7, 1760. John watched the crew sweat under a broiling Caribbean sun as they loaded barrels of sugar and casks of rum. Captain Benson cast off soon and sailed up Chesapeake Bay and the Rappahannock River to the bustling port of Fredericksburg, Virginia.

John's brother, William, owned a successful tailor shop in town. He stayed with William for three months until *Friendship* sailed to England in August with a cargo of tobacco, pig iron, and barrel staves. Younger scheduled one round trip a year for each of his ships, so John was home for Christmas. He returned to Virginia in the summers of 1762 and 1763.

John loved America from the first day he saw it. He used the visits to polish his social skills. Fredericksburg's most important citizens patronized William's shop. John studied their garments, manners, and conversations while they were being measured and fitted for new clothes. He worked hard to lose his Scottish country-boy accent.

Reverend Hogg had taught him to appreciate a good education. John practiced reading and writing, but, like many people of his day, he never learned to spell very well. While in Virginia, he studied celestial navigation, using the stars to determine where he was and where he wanted to go. He learned how to guide a ship anywhere on a cloudless night.

His third trip back to Whitehaven ended with a surprise. Younger had retired after losing money in a business decline. He released John from his remaining four years of apprenticeship. At only seventeen, John was a seasoned, independent crewman with four voyages under his belt.

In 1764, John became third mate in the crew of *King George*, a British slave ship from Whitehaven. After two years, he took a promotion to chief mate on the slaver *Two Friends*. The fifty-foot vessel had a crew of six and a cargo of "77 Negroes from Africa."[2] His second voyage on *Two Friends*, carrying rum to Africa and slaves to the Caribbean, was too much for John. He could no longer tolerate the cruelty he saw and the wretched conditions the slaves endured. He resigned when the ship reached Jamaica.

Taking Charge

After leaving *Two Friends*, John encountered Samuel McAdams, captain of *John* and a friend from

The Triangle Trade
Slaves were bought by European traders in Africa and taken to the West Indies and America's Southern colonies. There, they worked as field hands on sugar, cotton, and tobacco plantations. The crops were sold or traded to Europe, in return for manufactured goods. These items were then traded in Africa for more slaves. This system became known as the Triangle Trade.

Kirkcudbright. McAdams offered him a free trip home. During the voyage, McAdams and his first mate died of malaria. *John*'s seven-man crew did not know how to navigate, so the ship drifted aimlessly. John Paul took charge and sailed it safely into Kirkcudbright. The grateful owners appointed him captain for its next voyage to America.

At twenty-one, Captain John Paul was gaining greater responsibilities in the merchant marine. His experience and navigational skills made him a valuable employee. *John* was a small vessel and John Paul worked long hours. He oversaw the ship's operations and alternated standing watch with two mates. He bought and sold cargoes of rum, tobacco, wood, spices, and other goods in ports along his route. He dressed like a gentleman, was well-groomed, and tried to set a good example for the crew.

John Paul's next cruise to the Caribbean sailed for Tobago in the Windward Islands. The trip did not go well. In May 1770, the ship's carpenter, Mungo Maxwell, tried to lead the crew to mutiny. John Paul ended the illegal rebellion and ordered that Maxwell be flogged. Crewmen tied him to the rigging, where his bare back felt the severe pain from leather lashes cutting into his skin.

When *John* landed in Tobago, Maxwell went to the Vice-Admiralty Court, the office that ruled on crimes committed at sea. Maxwell filed a complaint against John Paul, showing his scars from the flogging to prove his maltreatment. The judges examined him before deciding that Captain John Paul was right and Maxwell's wounds were not extreme. Maxwell left for home on the *Barcelona Packet*. During the voyage, he died of typhoid fever.

When *John* arrived in Kirkcudbright, the sheriff charged John Paul with Maxwell's murder and imprisoned him. John Paul convinced the court that he would be willing to stand trial after he had gathered evidence from the West Indies to prove his innocence. The judge released him on bail and gave him time to collect the evidence.

Almost no one in Kirkcudbright believed that Paul was guilty. To encourage him, his friend James Smith sponsored him for the honor of membership in a fraternal organization called the Masons. Paul's nomination went to the Master, Wardens and Brethren of Free and Accepted Masons of the St. Bernard Lodge of Kirkcudbright.[3] They installed him as a member on

 *John Paul Jones*

November 27, 1770. He looked forward to meeting Masons in other parts of the world.

Trouble at Sea

John was sold in the spring of 1771. As a result, John Paul lost his job. He returned to Tobago the following year to take statements from James Simpson of the Vice-Admiralty Court and James Eastment, captain of *Barcelona Packet*, the ship on which Mungo Maxwell had died. Both confirmed that Maxwell had been in good health when he sailed for London, noting that he became ill and died from a fever. When Paul returned to London in September 1772, he sent the Maxwell documents to his mother, who gave them to the court. The judge accepted them, dismissed the murder charge, and cleared Paul's record.

Masons

Masonry, also called the Freemasons, is among the world's oldest Protestant organizations of brotherhood. It was started by tenth-century stoneworkers who were building cathedrals in Europe. Its secret rituals have made the association unpopular at times. Masonry's modern history began at the Grand Lodge of England in 1717. Many of the world's most influential people, especially in John Paul's time, were Masons. Well-known Masons included George Washington, Benjamin Franklin, and Wolfgang Amadeus Mozart.

20

In October 1772, the owners of the British merchant ship *Betsy* hired Paul as captain. It sailed between London and Tobago, with stops in Ireland and the island of Madeira, off the northwest coast of Africa. His skill in buying and selling various cargoes made the voyages successful financially.

John Paul was then twenty-five years old. His future was evolving and he no longer considered life at sea the ideal career. He had mastered every aspect of sailing, ships, and navigation. He had a sizable bank account and a thriving partnership with Archibald Stuart, a Tobago merchant-planter. Paul began thinking of getting married and buying a plantation, perhaps in America.

Betsy sailed from Plymouth, England, in January 1773. Problems plagued the voyage and Paul had to take the ship to Cork, Ireland, for repairs. While there, he became very ill and recovered slowly. Five months later, he was ready to leave for the Caribbean with *Betsy*'s cargo of potatoes, oats, claret wine, and sixty-five-pound kegs of butter.

After arriving in Tobago, Paul sold the cargo and arranged to buy another to take back to England. However, his life quickly changed forever with what he later called "the greatest misfortune of my life."[4]

Betsy's repairs had cost the ship's owners a lot of money. Paul hesitated to pay the crew while in Tobago because he knew they would waste the money ashore. He proposed, instead, to use their money to buy extra cargo and pay the men after selling it in England. The

This engraving shows John Paul Jones as a young man.

sailors, especially those from Tobago, resented the idea.

In an act of mutiny, one crewman urged the others to demand their wages immediately. They refused Paul's offer of free items from the ship's supply locker instead of money. The troublemaker began lowering the ship's rowboat to go ashore without permission. When he was ordered to stop, he rushed toward Paul forcing him to retreat to his cabin. There, Paul grabbed a sword and hurried back on deck.

The burly troublemaker yelled and ran at the captain again, swinging a club over Paul's head. Paul clutched his sword and thrust his arm forward to protect himself. The troublemaker lunged and Paul's sword plunged deep into his body. The man dropped to the deck and died.

Paul rowed ashore to find a justice of the peace and offer to surrender. He learned that he could remain free until a judge was available because Tobago had no authority over a crime at sea. However, his friends begged him to escape while he could. It was against his nature to run away, but he knew they were right.

He borrowed a horse, crossed the island, and found a ship preparing to leave Tobago for Barbados. With fifty British pounds (a type of currency) in his pocket, John Paul left behind everything he had worked so hard to build—his career, bank account, properties, friends, and business ventures.

3

THE CONTINENTAL NAVY

J ohn Paul led a mysterious life for nearly two years
after he escaped from Tobago. He went by the alias
of John Jones, lived quietly, and did not discuss his
past. He may have gone to Virginia when his brother
died in 1774. William left all his property to their wid-
owed sister, Mary Ann Lowden, in Scotland.

Many wealthy landowners in Virginia and the
Carolinas were Masons. John Paul met Robert Smith,
brother of James Smith, who had sponsored Paul for
membership in the Masons in Kirkcudbright years earlier. Smith introduced Paul to Joseph Hewes, a North
Carolina merchant and shipowner. Hewes and Paul
became close friends. Dr. John K. Read, founder of
Virginia's Grand Lodge of the Masons, was another
friend. Read was American patriot Benjamin Franklin's

nephew by marriage and a friend of Thomas Jefferson, another prominent American politician. Jefferson once carried Read's letters to John Paul in Philadelphia.

John Paul was in Philadelphia in September 1775. The air there was full of talk about Great Britain's government and King George III. Revolutionary ideas spread amid heated debates in every town and tavern. Resistance to unfair British taxation had hardened into defiance of the law in some places. Rebels who called themselves patriots aimed to cut all ties with Great Britain, while a small colonial population wanted the situation to stay the way it was. Most people preferred to remain loyal British subjects. They did, however, hope for lower taxes and less interference in their lives from Great Britain's legislature, known as Parliament.

Representatives of the thirteen American colonies convened the First Continental Congress in 1774, in Philadelphia. The purpose of this meeting was to find a way to settle the problems between America and Great Britain. In April 1775, a clash occurred between a few hundred British soldiers and the local militiamen in Lexington and Concord, Massachusetts. America's destiny changed forever as news of the fighting spread far and wide. The Second Continental Congress, which met that same year, soon became a government for the colonies as they began their fight for independence from Great Britain.

By July 1775, General George Washington, who had been named commander in chief of America's army, believed the colonies could not win an expanding war without sea power. Great Britain's Royal Navy

The Continental Congresses

These bodies, which eventually became a formal legislature, governed the colonies before, during, and after the Revolutionary War. The first Congress met from September 5 to October 26, 1774. It petitioned the British Parliament to ease colonial problems by changing some of the laws, especially tax laws, that Americans found unfair. The second Congress opened on May 10, 1775. Its main issue was to debate the possibility of America declaring independence from Great Britain. It also took charge of organizing the armed forces for the war.

had many ships manned by trained officers and men. Washington needed to stop the flow of military supplies, arms, and gunpowder to enemy troops and prevent British raiders from attacking and burning towns along America's coast.

Congress Establishes the Navy

In late summer, the Rhode Island legislature passed and sent to Congress a resolution declaring the urgent need for an American fleet. Partly because of General Washington's efforts and Rhode Island's resolution, Congress formed the Continental Navy on October 30, 1775. Seven congressmen formed a Naval Committee to oversee the new organization. The committee included four New Englanders and three

Southerners, among them John Paul's friend Joseph Hewes.

Six weeks later, on November 10, 1775, the Naval Committee formed the Marine Corps as part of the navy. Known as Sea Soldiers, marines had been part of navies for thousands of years. They provided armed protection, maintained discipline aboard ship, prevented mutinies, and led landing parties ashore.

Congress debated details of the navy's structure and responsibilities for two months. Representative John Adams of Massachusetts was deeply involved in the planning. He considered the navy essential to America's war effort. He argued with Samuel Chase of Maryland, who worried about money and was convinced that building a fleet was "the maddest idea in the world."[1]

Around this time, John Paul changed his name again. He had been calling himself "John Jones" since leaving Tobago. He considered "Jones" a common name, and knowing that "John Paul Jones" was unlikely to attract much attention, he decided to resume using his real name with the new last name "Jones."

Jones hoped to join the new navy. He asked Joseph Hewes to help him win an appointment. Hewes knew Jones had a thorough knowledge of seamanship, having learned from the best men in the British merchant marine. Jones knew all the routes between England and the West Indies, and best of all, he was not afraid of the British.

The Naval Committee had been told to create a seagoing fighting force out of practically nothing. The

men had a hard time making decisions because the committee's members kept changing. Representatives came and went, served on several other congressional committees, attended meetings day and night, and worst of all, had no practical naval experience.

The Continental Navy's missions were intended to defend America's coastlines and commercial shipping as well as carry cargo and correspondence. The Naval Committee had little money to buy ships and pay salaries. It ordered the construction of thirteen new

The Continental Navy used the slogan "Don't Tread on Me" on its first flag in 1775. The United States Marine Corps painted the rattlesnake's image on their drums.

frigates, which would take years to complete. There were few officers and men to sail the ships. Because time was short, the committee leased or borrowed privately owned armed merchant ships. It hired experienced officers from the merchant marine and filled crews with anyone the captains could recruit.

The First American Naval Squadron

On November 5, 1775, Esek Hopkins, who had forty years of experience, became commodore of the first squadron in America's Continental Navy. His flagship, *Alfred*, was the largest of seven armed vessels in a squadron known as Hopkins's Fleet. The others were *Andrea Doria, Columbus, Providence, Hornet, Wasp,* and *Cabot.*[2] Hopkins's son, John, was captain of *Cabot*, and his brother, Stephen, was chairman of the Naval Committee.

Commodore Hopkins asked John Paul Jones to raise America's new Grand Union flag aboard *Alfred*, the first Continental Navy ship to fly it. The event

The Grand Union Flag

Philadelphia hat maker Margaret Manny sewed the Grand Union flag from 101 yards of bunting and charged the expense to *Alfred*'s account.[3] The flag's red and white stripes represented the thirteen original colonies. The Union Jack in the upper left quadrant affirmed Great Britain's importance in the creation of America.

Commodore Esek Hopkins was John Paul Jones's first commanding officer. They served aboard the flagship Alfred, *and Jones was second in command.*

occurred at dockside in Philadelphia, where Jones was involved with *Alfred*'s conversion from merchant ship to warship. He later said, "I hoisted with my own hands, the Flag of Freedom the first time it was displayed, on the Alfred, on the Delaware. . . ."[4]

Congressman Hewes encouraged the navy to grant its initial appointment as first lieutenant to John Paul Jones. It did so on December 7, 1775. Jones assumed three weeks of duty as captain of *Alfred* until its permanent captain could take command. Dudley Saltonstall arrived from Rhode Island on December 23 to join Hopkins aboard *Alfred*. Ten years older than Jones, Saltonstall was a master mariner and a descendent of three of New England's first families. Jones disliked him immediately, considering him a snob.

Before Jones joined *Alfred*, Hewes had offered him command of *Providence*, but Jones declined. He believed he would learn more seamanship as second in command to the commodore. Jones did not foresee the navy's becoming a strong military force, nor did he expect America to declare its independence from Great Britain. Like many immigrants, he considered himself a "citizen of the world" who believed in liberty for its own sake. Jones did not share America's patriotic zeal at that time.

Hopkins's squadron left Philadelphia on January 4, 1776, and became icebound in the Delaware River for two weeks. Officers stood twenty-four-hour watches to prevent crewmen from growing restless and deserting the ship. Jones kept them busy by training them in the use of *Alfred*'s guns.

The Squadron Goes to Sea

Hopkins received orders on January 5, 1776, to search and destroy enemy vessels in Chesapeake Bay and along the Carolina coast. Afterward, he was to sail north to Rhode Island and take prizes in Narragansett Bay. The orders had a loophole. They stated that, if bad weather or other problems arose, he could follow "such Courses as your best Judgment shall Suggest to you. . . ."[5]

After the weather cleared, Hopkins decided to take advantage of the loophole and bypass Chesapeake Bay. The squadron left on February 14 for a fast sail to the Caribbean to capture gunpowder and weapons for Washington's army. Hopkins and Saltonstall were familiar with the route from their days in the merchant marine. They arrived at New Providence Island in the Bahamas two weeks later. There was no civilian resistance because Great Britain had withdrawn its army regiment from the fort in the town of Nassau.

The expedition was almost a disaster. Hopkins did not keep the squadron out of sight when, on March 2, he sent navy crewmen and United States marines into Nassau Harbor to surprise the town. The governor ordered cannon fire from the fort to ward off the American landing party. That night, island residents removed one hundred fifty barrels of gunpowder, leaving Hopkins two dozen barrels, eighty-eight cannons, and fifteen mortars.[6] The trip was a partial success, but Hopkins had hoped to find more gunpowder.

The squadron sailed on March 17, 1776, for Block Island, Rhode Island, and arrived three weeks later.

The frigate Alfred *rides at anchor in the harbor, with sails furled to reveal the complex rigging on its three masts.*

Cannons

Cannons were warships' most damaging weapons. They shot iron balls of various weights and sizes that could destroy the wooden decks, frames, and masts of enemy ships. Cannons also shot pieces of jagged metal into the air to shred enemy ships' sails and riggings, and they fired flammable shells to set entire villages ablaze.

Cannons rolled back because of recoil action after being fired. Heavy ropes and noisy wooden tackles were needed to control and move the cannons for firing. Crewmen pushed cannons forward until the barrels extended beyond the porthole before firing.

Shortly after midnight on April 6, it encountered the British ship H.M.S. *Glasgow*. The British captain, Tryingham Howe, did not recognize the enemy ship immediately. The American squadron went on alert and waited for Hopkins's signal to form a line of battle, which did not come. Instead, he allowed each captain to make his own decision. *Glasgow* closed within pistol range of *Cabot*, hailing for identification. *Cabot*'s response went unheard because an American marine tossed a hand grenade onto *Glasgow*'s deck.

The resulting battle lasted an hour and a half. Outnumbered five to one, *Glasgow* shot two rounds of cannon fire, wounding Hopkins and killing several Americans. Another round disabled *Cabot*, which drifted away. *Columbia* entered the fight late because other ships' sails blanketed the wind and it could not maneuver. *Andrea Doria* avoided several collisions and *Providence* never fought at all.

In the confusion, Captain Howe expected the Americans to board *Glasgow* at any minute. Its hull had suffered several rounds of cannon fire and its sails and riggings were in shreds. Howe withdrew and sailed for Newport, Rhode Island. Hopkins signaled the squadron to collect the damaged *Cabot* and depart.

Congress and the newspapers praised the Commodore's victory. His officers and men were disgusted. Jones agreed with Captain Nicholas Biddle of *Andrea Doria*, who said, "a more imprudent, ill conducted Affair never happened."[7] Jones wrote to Joseph Hewes that, if officers were to be obeyed, they had to be worthy of respect.

Hopkins offered Jones a second chance to command *Providence*, this time with a temporary promotion to captain. Jones accepted. He had come to believe that America could support a professional navy, both politically and financially. If independence came, a long war could follow. Jones wanted to be part of it.

$\boxed{4}$

PROVIDENCE

Three months after taking command on May 10, 1776, the Naval Committee selected Jones for the permanent rank of captain. This enhanced his satisfaction with *Providence* and its fine crew. He had learned to appreciate the sloop and the way it caught the wind in its enormous sail, racing through the sea with ease, leaving a long, bubbling wake.

Jones's first order was to ferry Continental Army officers and men from Boston, Massachusetts, to General Washington's headquarters in New York. After routine troop-and-cargo trips between New York and New England, he escorted a merchant fleet from Boston to Philadelphia.

Congressman Joseph Hewes welcomed Jones to town and introduced him to the Marine Committee,

formerly called the Naval Committee. Jones met Congressman Robert Morris of Pennsylvania and John Hancock, the Marine Committee chairman. Jones liked Morris and asked to correspond with him, as he had done with Hewes for some time. Jones was clever and ambitious. He knew that, without any family or business connections to advance his career, it would be helpful to have the support of influential friends.

First Independent Cruise

In early August, the Marine Committee granted Jones's request for an independent cruise. His orders were to "Seize, take, Sink, Burn or destroy" enemy ships.[1] He was to decide when he departed, where he would go, and how long he would be gone. Offered a choice of two vessels, he stayed with *Providence*. He liked the crew and the way the ship sailed.

The Marine Committee gave Jones a list of vessels that could and could not become prizes. Congress had decreed on March 23, 1776, that ships and cargoes owned by British citizens, or those ferrying goods to British armies, could be captured. The committee provided names of Continental agents in each state who would help Jones sell the prizes he captured. If he received confidential or political information about the military, he was to visit the nearest port and send a report to the Marine Committee. He was to protect and assist American vessels, represent the navy well, and treat prisoners kindly.

Within days, *Providence* began a forty-nine-day cruise. Jones enjoyed not having anyone aboard to give

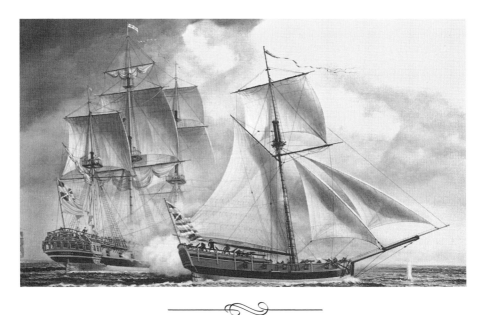

A single-masted sloop of war like the Providence *engaged in combat at sea with a much larger square-rigger.*

him orders. After a successful beginning, he sent several prizes to American ports. This, however, left him short of crewmen. He resolved the situation by convincing more than two dozen British prisoners to join his crew. Sailors on both sides of the war sometimes opted to join the enemy rather than remain in prison. Most crewmen were more interested in the money they might make than in politics.

Jones encountered H.M.S. *Solebay* near Bermuda on September 20, 1776. The British frigate chased *Providence* for ten and a half hours before coming close enough to hoist the American flag, trying to trick Jones. *Solebay* fired its guns to leeward, away from the wind, in a traditional sign of friendship. Jones was not

fooled. He knew the Continental Navy did not have such a ship. *Providence* darted across *Solebay*'s bow, almost daring it to follow. The slow British ship and its crew could only watch as the enemy sped away into the night.

In mid-September, Jones concluded that most British ships had left Bermuda. He sailed north to Nova Scotia, Canada, seeking prizes, men, and wood for repairs. On September 22, several local fishermen agreed to join his crew. As he left the area, Jones burned an English schooner, sank a second, and captured a third.

His new crewmen told Jones that there was a cluster of boats at the nearby harbor of Ile Madame, Nova Scotia. The Americans arrived to surprise the local fishermen, who surrendered immediately. Jones did not have enough men to sail the captured ships, so he bargained with his prisoners. He gave them two prize schooners, *Betty* and *Hope*, for their help in preparing the other prizes to be sold.

Navy Politics

Providence returned to Narragansett Bay, Rhode Island, after forty-nine days. Jones considered it his most enjoyable cruise. Before sailing again, he wrote to Robert Morris about the competition between the navy and privateers to recruit good crewmen. Jones worried about the future. He emphasized to Morris, "without a Respectable Navy—alas America!"[2]

Jones lobbied the government to give navy crews bigger shares of the prize money they captured. He

Privateers

Privateers were privately owned, armed merchant ships. When compared with the navy, privateer crews were paid almost twice as much, took shorter voyages, and faced less discipline and danger at sea. About two thousand privateers supplemented the Continental Navy after Great Britain convinced some Europeans not to do business with the colonies. The Second Continental Congress granted written licenses, called letters of marque and reprisal, authorizing privately owned ships to attack, capture, or sink British merchant ships. Privateers kept all the prize money for ships they captured.

told Morris that the British Navy gave all prize money to its officers and crewmen. He asked how America could do less, and Congress agreed. In mid-October 1776, the share for certain ships was increased from one third to one half, with the rest going to Congress. The change helped, but debate over the details dragged on for months.

Jones also pushed the Marine Committee to give pay raises to officers, who earned less than their British counterparts. Meanwhile, American seamen received more money to serve one year than did British crewmen, who had to stay on until the war was over.

Back to *Alfred*

Jones became captain of *Alfred* in October 1776. He received three assignments immediately. First, Hopkins ordered him to free Americans who had been imprisoned by the British in the coal mines at Cape Breton, Nova Scotia. Second, Jones was to intercept a fleet of colliers, or coal carriers, bringing fuel to the British Army in New York. Third, if weather permitted, he was to destroy Great Britain's fishing grounds in the North Atlantic.

Alfred sailed from Providence, Rhode Island, on October 27 with one hundred forty officers and men. Its companion vessel, *Hampton*, hit a submerged rock before leaving Narragansett Bay and had to return to port. Its captain, Hoystead Hacker, and a crew of seventy-five transferred to *Providence* and sailed with *Alfred* on November 1. *Providence* began leaking after a powerful storm and the crew wanted to go home. They slipped away one night during a downpour and returned to port.

Jones captured three British colliers, but not the ones he had been sent to find. His prisoners reported that the Americans he was supposed to rescue from the coal mines at Cape Breton had joined the British Navy.

Jones's favorite prize from the voyage was *Mellish*, an armed transport ship he captured on November 12. Its cargo included winter uniforms and supplies for the British Army. Jones put Lieutenant Philip Brown aboard *Mellish* with orders to stay within signaling distance. They could not risk losing this precious windfall needed by General Washington's troops in New Brunswick, New Jersey.

On December 8, *Alfred* encountered the British ship H.M.S. *Milford* and a crew of two hundred near Cape Cod, Massachusetts. British Captain Burr assumed *Alfred* was friendly. He mistook it for H.M.S. *Flora*, the collier escort Jones had tried unsuccessfully to find. Jones knew *Alfred* would be overmatched in a

Captain Jones is framed in the elaborate French fashion popular during the reign of King Louis XVI.

fight, so he came up with a plan. He attached a bright lantern to *Alfred*'s mast and ordered his prize masters to stay on course, no matter what Jones did. He wanted to mislead *Milford*'s captain by sailing toward New York and then changing course abruptly, allowing the prizes to escape unnoticed.

Captain Burr became suspicious around midnight. He knew British ships bound for New York would not turn away suddenly. *Milford* and *Alfred* pursued each other all morning. Shortly before noon, Jones was close enough to fire his cannons. He ordered a prize master, Midshipman Robert Sanders, to drop behind *Milford* to compare the size and number of its cannons with *Alfred*'s. While Sanders did so, Jones found an unexpected chance to escape and took it. *Milford* quickly captured Sanders and his prize.

Jones had a good voyage, although he regretted losing Sanders. He knew he could not have rescued him and saved the prizes, too. *Mellish* was an especially important prize. Everyone made good money from selling its cargo. Jones was glad to learn that the supply of heavyweight uniforms reached General Washington in time for the Battle of Trenton on the night of Christmas, 1776. Midshipman Sanders went to prison in Nova Scotia. For there, he contacted Commodore Hopkins and protested that Jones had let him down in a crisis.

Navy Promotion

Personal problems interfered with Jones's career at times and they were often his fault. He was very

competitive and had trouble controlling his temper. Jones also criticized fellow officers unfairly and hesitated to praise his crews, which often made them feel unappreciated. American statesman Benjamin Franklin told him that, if he rewarded his men more often and more generously, he would become a great captain.

Congress and Jones's friends were tired of his complaints about naval ranks. Because the navy had been formed hastily, and war followed immediately, there had not been time to develop a foolproof system of promoting worthy officers. Jones resented the existing system, feeling he and other good officers were not being recognized.

Congress tried to improve its method of ranking. At the request of the Marine Committee, Congress took action on October 10, 1776. It published a list of captains and assigned each one a ship to command. The men were ranked according to the dates they had received their current permanent rank. The resolution required that, after October 10, 1777, officers would be promoted according to the dates they received their naval commissions.

Joseph Hewes was absent when Congress compiled the list. Despite Hewes's support when Jones received the navy's first lieutenant appointment in 1775, Jones was ranked number eighteen out of twenty-six captains on the new list. He was reassigned to *Providence*.

Jones was enraged. He considered the list a product of political and personal favoritism. However, Congress had good reasons for the decision. The navy had ordered thirteen new frigates in 1775. Each was

Officers' Ranks and Promotions

A commissioned officer was promoted according to how long he had been in the navy and the date of his most recent previous promotion. An assignment to a ship was based on date of rank. An officer with longer service was senior to one with less service time, regardless of his actual experience at sea or his age.

to be ported in the town where it would be built. Congress paired each builder with a captain from the area. Both men were to be well-known in their community. A good reputation helped to recruit a crew, especially in times when men were not eager to sign up.

As an immigrant, Jones had friends everywhere, but no strong link to any one place. He believed his lack of "insider" connections hurt him. However, Jones was not out of favor. John Hancock of the Marine Committee wrote to Robert Morris, "I admire the spirited conduct of . . . Jones . . . I know he does not love to be idle."[3]

Morris tried to comply with Hancock's hint. In February 1777, he informed Jones of a plan to take the war to British soil. Morris wrote, "our Infant fleet cannot protect our own Coasts; and the only effectual relief it can afford us is to attack the enemies [British] defenseless places and . . . oblige them to station more of their ships in their own Countries . . ."[4]

Stars and Stripes

In addition to Jones's appointment to the *Ranger*, a second resolution was issued on June 14, 1777. Congress resolved: "That the flag of the United States be made of thirteen stripes, alternate red and white; that the union be thirteen stars, white in a blue field, representing a new Constellation."[5]

On June 14, 1777, Congress resolved to appoint John Paul Jones captain of the frigate *Ranger*, which was then under construction in Portsmouth, New Hampshire. The previously assigned captain, John Roche, had been accused of trafficking in stolen goods and fired from his job. Jones learned of his new command on the same day the Stars and Stripes became America's new flag.

5

RANGER

Jones arrived in Portsmouth, New Hampshire, in mid-July 1777 to oversee *Ranger*'s final construction. He lived in a private home on State Street and made good friends among the Masons of Saint John Lodge and their families.

The Marine Committee had ordered a ship from builder John Langdon a year earlier. He was to provide "with the utmost expedition a . . . Vessel of War."[1] No design had been specified, so Langdon adapted existing plans and gathered ideas from his builders.

Portsmouth was surrounded by forests of tall trees that were used for making decks and masts. The Langdon shipyard finished *Ranger* in only four months. The ship had a festive launch on May 10 and was then

moved to Rindges Wharf to complete the interior and install masts, riggings, and sails.

John Langdon

Langdon was the agent representing the navy's business in Portsmouth. He and Jones worked together, but they often clashed. Jones wanted the best of everything for *Ranger*, and he complained when he did not get it. Langdon saw Jones as a perfectionist, while Jones considered Langdon uncooperative.

They argued over *Ranger*'s sails. Good sailcloth was expensive and hard to find. Langdon had bought 422 yards of canvas from Christian Starbuck of Nantucket, Massachusetts, months before Jones arrived.[2] When *Ranger*'s sails were finished in October, half the fabric was canvas and the other half was of a poor-quality fabric called hessian, or burlap. Jones was angry and he blamed Langdon.

Jones knew at a glance that *Ranger*'s masts were too tall and heavy for the ship's weight. This would affect the ship's stability at sea. Lacking time to change them, he temporarily removed two cannons to improve *Ranger*'s center of gravity. Jones had the ship's hull painted black with a yellow stripe. He often used his own money for extra expenses.

Congressman William Whipple of New Hampshire, Langdon, and Jones were appointed to select *Ranger*'s officers. Whipple and Langdon chose their friends and relatives. They rebuffed Jones's suggestions, except for his close friend Marine Captain Matthew Parke

GREAT
ENCOURAGEMENT
FOR
SEAMEN.

LL GENTLEMEN SEAMEN and able-bodied LANDSMEN who have a Mind to diftinguifh themfelves in the GLORIOUS CAUSE of their COUNTRY, and make their Fortunes, an, Opportunity now offers on board the Ship RANGER, of Twenty Guns, (for FRANCE) now laying in PORTSMOUTH, in the State of NEW-HAMPSHIRE, commanded by JOHN PAUL JONES Efq; let them repair to the Ship's Rendezvous in PORTSMOUTH, or at the Sign of Commodore MANLEY, in SALEM, where they will be kindly entertained, and receive the greateft Encouragement.---The Ship RANGER, in the Opinion of every Perfon who has feen her is looked upon to be one of the beft Cruizers in AMERICA.---She will be always able to Fight her Guns under a moft excellent Cover ; and no Veffel yet built was ever calculated for failing fafter, and making good Weather.

Any GENTLEMEN VOLUNTEERS who have a Mind to take an agreable Voyage in this pleafant Seafon of the Year, may, by entering on board the above Ship RANGER, meet with every Civility they can poffibly expect, and for a further Encouragement depend on the firft Opportunity being embraced to reward each one agreable to his Merit.

All reafonable Travelling Expences will be allowed, and the Advance-Money be paid on their Appearance on Board.

IN CONGRESS, MARCH 29, 1777.

RESOLVED,

THAT the MARINE COMMITTEE be authorifed to advance to every able Seaman, that enters into the CONTINENTAL SERVICE, any Sum not exceeding FORTY DOLLARS, and to every ordinary Seaman or Landfman, any Sum not exceeding TWENTY DOLLARS, to be deducted from their future Prize-Money.

By Order of CONGRESS,

JOHN-HANCOCK, PRESIDENT.

DANVERS; Printed by E. RUSSELL, at the Houfe late the Bell-Tavern.

Jones placed posters everywhere to recruit Ranger's *crew. He competed with privateers, other navy ships, and the fact that most potential recruits could not read.*

and Parke's son, David Wendell, who was made a midshipman.

Jones had two disadvantages in recruiting a crew. He was not from the Portsmouth area, and he had to compete with other navy ships and privateers. He posted handbills and ran newspaper ads. Friends in other towns helped him. He held patriotic events featuring United States marines playing Scottish bagpipes and drums.

Ranger's First Voyage

By November 1, *Ranger* had enlisted a crew of 145 men and six officers.[3] With congressional approval, Jones guaranteed each crewman a portion of his wage in advance. Congress did not promise the crew money for captured prizes, but Jones implied that this was probable.

Before sailing, Jones told friends that his crew was the best in the world. Still, *Ranger* and its men were unproven, so Jones wrote his will, naming Joseph Hewes and Robert Morris as executors. He left everything he had to his mother and sisters in Scotland, with whom he kept in touch through letters.

Ranger sailed from Portsmouth on November 1, 1777, and arrived in Paimboeuf, France, on December 2. Jones carried dispatches for America's commissioners in Paris. These messages reported the surrender of British General John Burgoyne on October 17, 1777, after the Battle of Saratoga, New York. Jones wanted to be first to bring the news, but the French vessel

Penet had docked hours earlier and a courier was already en route to Paris.

Jones remained in Paimboeuf for two weeks to refit *Ranger*. Crewmen replaced the hessian sails with new canvas, careened the bottom, shortened the masts, and added thirty tons of rocks below decks for ballast (heavy material used to add stability). The changes repositioned *Ranger*'s center of gravity to prevent it from leaning too far in a strong wind. If this happened, water could pour into the gunports, ruin the gunpowder, and perhaps sink the ship.

While in port, Jones provided his crew with fresh food and drink. He also arranged a boat for trips ashore, and loaned the men money from his own pocket. Although he could be demanding, and not always tactful, the captain upheld his responsibility to take care of his men.

Careening

Wooden ships were careened twice yearly and more often in warm waters. After removing portable items, masts, and sails, the crew used ropes and pulleys to roll the ship over and expose the bottom. They scraped off sea creatures that had attached themselves and bored holes into the wooden hull. The men applied a mixture of fine crude oil and sticky pitch that hardened into a seal in seawater. Then they rolled the boat upright and reinstalled the equipment.

L'Indien and European Politics

The Marine Committee had asked John Paul Jones to take *Ranger* to France. After arriving, he expected to take command of *L'Indien*, a ship being built in Amsterdam, Holland, for the American commissioners. Jones learned that Great Britain's supporters in Holland had been pressuring that government to sell *L'Indien* to France. The supporters insisted that, if it went to America, the Dutch would be violating their neutral position in Great Britain's war with America.

The American commissioners confused the situation by continually asking their government for money. The Dutch concluded that America could not afford to buy *L'Indien*. Jones went to Paris to discuss the matter with Commissioner Benjamin Franklin. After seeing Franklin, he called upon Monsieur Gabrielle Sartine, France's minister of marine. Sartine made no promises about *L'Indien*'s future or her command.

Franklin and Jones became very good friends and began to correspond. The commissioner, always a great admirer of women, introduced the captain to influential ladies and gentlemen, who welcomed him. Franklin worked hard behind the scenes, coaxing France to acknowledge America's independence publicly. This would benefit the American Navy greatly.

In January 1778, commissioners Franklin and Silas Deane ordered Jones to proceed "in the manner . . . best for distressing the Enemies of the United States . . ."[4] Until then, America had not attacked British commerce ashore. Jones told Franklin about a letter he had received from Robert Morris the year before, stating that, "Destroying their settlements [villages]—spreading alarms . . . will oblige them to defend their extensive possessions . . . [this] is of . . . more consequence . . . than all the Plunder."[5]

Jones wanted the British to experience firsthand the same kind of devastation their army was causing in America. He intended to raid their towns and destroy their ships at home. Franklin approved Jones's plan to "put an end of burnings in America by making a good fire in England of *Shipping*."[6]

A Salute From France

Ranger and its sister ship, *Independence*, left Paimboeuf for training at sea, arriving in Quiberon Bay in France on February 13. A large French fleet, commanded by Admiral LaMotte Piquet was waiting there to escort American merchant ships to sea. Aboard his flagship, *Le Bretagne*, the admiral agreed to Jones's

British Burnings

British soldiers and marines had set fire to America's coastal towns for years. They torched houses, crops, and woodlands, killed animals, terrified families, and left destruction in their wake. On March 8, 1778, the British government instructed that, barring a victory over General Washington, the army's policy would be to "seize or destroy every Ship . . . all Wharfs and Stores, and Materials for Ship-Building . . ."[7]

In this 1898 painting by Edward Moran, the new American flag, Stars and Stripes, flown by U.S.S. Ranger, *receives a nine-gun salute from the French fleet in Quiberon Bay, on February 14, 1778.*

request for an exchange of ceremonial salutes. The privilege was usually reserved for more senior officers.

Ranger and *Independence* sailed past *Le Bretagne* at six o'clock in the evening of February 14. *Ranger* fired thirteen guns to honor Admiral LaMotte Piquet. *Le Bretagne* responded with nine salvos, but not to honor Jones. Instead, France's salute represented the first official recognition of America's Stars and Stripes by a foreign government at sea. Jones may not have known that the gesture also acknowledged France's secret alliance with America, signed one week earlier.

This original portfolio cover combines images of Jones, Ranger, *and the Stars and Stripes as they were together in France at Quiberon Bay on February 14, 1778.*

Jones sailed for weeks in French waters between Quiberon Bay and Brest, studying tides, weather, and landmarks. The crew worked well together, but they disliked the captain's strict discipline. His main problems on the voyage were crew desertions and cases of smallpox, a serious disease.

Ranger and England

Jones sailed to England's west coast in April and soon found a hidden cove from which he could stir up trouble. On April 19, in the North Channel between Scotland and Ireland, an Irish fisherman volunteered some valuable information. The British warship H.M.S. *Drake* was anchored in Belfast Bay at Carrickfergus, Ireland.

Jones found *Drake* the next day. He outlined to his crew a plan to charge into the harbor under full sail and start firing. They vetoed it. Jones finally convinced them to surprise *Drake* by sailing into Belfast Bay at night, with gunports closed, appearing to be a peaceful merchant ship. *Ranger* would cross *Drake*'s bow, drop the anchor to slow down, and fire cannons along *Drake*'s hull. Then, the crew would climb aboard for hand-to-hand fighting.

The plan seemed straightforward. However, after *Ranger* entered the harbor, the anchor chain became wedged and could not be released in time to begin the plan. The British never noticed as Jones, a hundred feet away, glided past them in the dark.

Heavy winds the next night prevented another attempt to seize *Drake*. Jones cruised near Whitehaven, the port where his sea-faring career began, and he decided to launch an attack from there. His men were not interested. They wanted prize money. *Ranger* had only captured three prizes, thus far, during the voyage. Jones had scuttled, or sunk, other captives because he did not consider them worth keeping.

Jones tried to be diplomatic with the crew. He had good reason to suspect First Lieutenant Thomas Simpson of provoking defiance. Simpson, who was John Langdon's brother-in-law, resented Jones. He had expected to command *Ranger* himself. A Swedish officer, Lieutenant Jean Meijer, warned Jones about whispers of rebellion. When Master David Cullam signaled to begin a mutiny, Jones put a pistol to the man's head to end the matter. After that, Jones remained on guard.

The Port of Whitehaven

On April 22, *Ranger* approached Whitehaven as the wind died down in Solway Firth, stranding the ship miles from town. Jones departed at midnight with two boats and thirty-one volunteers, who rowed three hours to reach the harbor at dawn.[8] They found two hundred to three hundred boats at anchor or on the beach.

Fortresses on the north and south sides guarded the harbor. Jones posted a sentry and divided the men into two groups. He sent one to burn ships on the north side. He took the other to the south, where they scaled the wall, tied up sleepy sentries, and spiked the

cannons. Jones and Midshipman Joe Green then went to spike the north side cannons.

Jones expected many ships to be on fire when he returned to the harbor. Instead, he found dark torches and burned out "candles" made of rolled canvas dipped in sulfur. Someone ran to light a torch at a nearby house. The flame, a candle, and a barrel of tar started a huge blaze aboard the collier *Thompson*.

A disloyal *Ranger* crewman, David Smith, awakened Whitehaven residents with his shouts of warning as he pounded on their doors. An angry crowd gathered at the harbor. Jones, pistol in hand, cautioned them to stay away. He stood between them and what he called the "Ship of Fire."[9] The raiders rowed back to *Ranger*, followed by fading voices and wayward gunfire.

Jones had planned to burn dozens of ships. When he did not get his chance, he wanted another bold strike. He decided to kidnap a rich nobleman to exchange for American sailors being held in British jails. He chose the Earl of Selkirk, who lived on Saint Mary's Isle in Kirkcudbright Bay, near Jones's birthplace.

He took two officers and a dozen armed men in a small boat. They told people they encountered that they were seeking young men for the Royal Navy. A gardener at the mansion said the earl was in Derbyshire, England. Having missed the earl, Jones turned to leave. Lieutenant Samuel Wallingford and Master David Cullam asked if the crew could rob Selkirk's mansion. They said Whitehaven and the kidnapping had yielded nothing, and the men needed a success. Jones agreed but decided to wait for them at the boat. He ordered them not to harm the Selkirks and to take only their silver.

Countess Selkirk

Within minutes, the earl's wife, her son, daughters, governess, butler, and guests had alarming visitors. Countess Selkirk assumed the unsavory characters around her mansion were pirates. She sent everyone upstairs except the butler and the governess. Then, she let the officers come in. They assured her that all would be well if she surrendered the silver.

The defenseless countess responded with grace. The men had not come prepared for a robbery, so she gave them cloth sacks into which they put the treasures. When David Cullam reviewed her written household inventory, he noticed that the coffee and tea pots were missing. She ordered the butler to bring them. She watched as her warm teapot, complete with wet tea leaves, disappeared into a sack.

The countess requested a written receipt, but there was not enough time. The officers accepted a glass of wine while the governess asked the crewmen waiting outside about life in America. The officers bade Countess Selkirk good-bye, joined their men, and left to meet Jones at the boat for the three-mile trip to *Ranger*. The entire episode took less than fifteen minutes.

6

PIRATE OR PATRIOT?

After raiding Whitehaven and Saint Mary's Isle,
Ranger cruised up the Scottish coast and across
the mouth of the North Channel. The events did little damage to the British, but the psychological impact
was enormous. Jones had dropped the Revolutionary
War right into England's lap, landing Americans on
British soil and confronting British people. He became a
folk hero in America, where newspapers printed every
tidbit about his exploits.

There was little doubt about what the British
thought. Most considered Jones a pirate and a
scoundrel. His reputation and deeds grew daily, fed by
fear and rumor. Angry letters of protest poured into
the headquarters of Great Britain's Royal Navy. Two
warships were sent to guard major shipping lanes.

Scotland

Kirkcudbright
Kirkbean

Carrickfergus
Belfast

Whitehaven

Ireland

Irish Sea

Wales

IRISH SEA
REGION

N
W · E
S

On Ranger's voyage in the spring of 1778, Jones continued to be unpredictable and stun the enemy. This map shows some of the places he visited during this wartime expedition.

Harbors near Whitehaven posted lookouts. Citizens bought gunpowder and cleaned their weapons, whether they worked or not, to protect themselves against Jones.

Ranger and *Drake*

British newspapers printed thousands of stories from supposed eyewitnesses who claimed to have seen the swarthy pirate captain and his motley crew. One report said *Ranger*'s former crewman, David Freeman, signed a sworn statement that Jones was captain of the so-called privateer *Ranger*. The London *Morning Post* of April 28, 1778, published his full name, John Paul Jones, for the first time.

Aboard *Ranger*, far from the frenzy, Jones pondered his next move. He remembered the near miss with H.M.S. *Drake* in Belfast Bay six days earlier, and he decided to try again.

Ranger approached the entrance to the bay on April 24 without flying identifying flags. *Drake* was already coming to investigate. Jones hid the crew below deck and ordered the helmsman, Samuel Stacey, to steer directly for the enemy. *Ranger* appeared harmless with its gunports shut. Jones hoped *Drake*'s captain could not count the cannons.

Drake sent a lieutenant to the *Ranger* in a small boat to ask about the newcomer. Jones invited him aboard and cordially took him prisoner. The deception delighted *Ranger*'s crew and diverted their attention from thoughts of mutiny over the small number of prizes they had captured thus far.

The original caption for this picture reads, "From a drawing taken from the Life, on board the Serapis." *It implies that John Paul Jones really dressed like a pirate and had stolen the ship.*

Pleasure boats anchored and bystanders lined the shore waiting to see the two warships in action. Only an hour of light remained, and the captains did not delay. When *Drake*'s lieutenant did not return, smoke alarms ashore alerted the crowd to move to a safe distance.

Jones lingered outside Belfast Bay, drawing *Drake* into mid-channel, where the ships could maneuver. He waited for the British to come closer. *Drake* raised the Union Jack. Jones hoisted the Stars and Stripes. *Drake*'s Captain Burden hailed for identification. Jones told Master David Cullam to reply, "The American Continental Ship *Ranger*."[1]

Jones ordered Stacey to cross *Drake*'s path while *Ranger*'s cannons fired on the enemy's bow. Jones did not try to put his men aboard. Instead, he targeted *Drake*'s men, masts, sails, and riggings, intending to save the hull as a prize. *Drake* was a good foe, in armaments and size, with a larger crew than *Ranger*.

Jones's log indicated "The Action was warm, close and obstinate."[2] It lasted an hour and five minutes. At the end, Captain Burden was dead and First Lieutenant Dobbs lay mortally wounded. *Drake*'s sails and riggings hung in shreds. Her senior crewman surrendered. *Ranger*'s gunfire ceased.

Among prisoners taken from *Drake* were 133 officers and men, including the cook and his wife.[3] Jones held burial services with full military honors for Burden and Dobbs. *Drake* could not sail until a crew had worked all night, trying to make it more seaworthy. *Ranger* took the ship in tow, with Lieutenant Simpson in command aboard *Drake*. Jones ordered him to stay within a certain distance of *Ranger* and pay close attention to Jones's signals. If the ships became separated, Simpson was to go to the military port at Brest, France.

The British Admiralty sent ships in all directions to look for Jones. He eluded them while news of the battle heightened Great Britain's fears. Everyone had an excuse to explain *Drake*'s defeat.

Ranger towed *Drake* around Northern Ireland and south toward the French coast. On May 4, Jones cut the tow rope and sailed away to pursue a potential prize. He hailed for Simpson to follow as best he could. Simpson and the others aboard *Drake* did not hear the order clearly. Simpson hailed *Ranger* to ask if he was supposed to leave for Brest. Lieutenant Elijah Hall on *Ranger*'s quarterdeck misunderstood Simpson's question and responded that he should.

Jones returned two days later to find that *Drake* was gone. He raised more sail for a fast and angry pursuit. When he caught up with Simpson, Jones did not believe that the lieutenant had not heard his order. Jones removed him from command for disobeying orders and put Lieutenant Hall aboard *Drake*.

Another Encounter With Countess Selkirk

Ranger returned to Brest on May 8. After long thoughts about Countess Selkirk, Jones wrote to her that day. The letter arrived within a month. He expressed admiration for her courtesy and hoped she was unharmed. He explained why his men took the

silver, and pledged to buy and return it to her when it was sold. Jones described the Whitehaven raid and the battle with *Drake*. He asked her to urge her husband to help end the devastating war Jones believed Great Britain could not win. He also requested help to arrange exchanges of American and British naval prisoners.

He ended with a plea for friendship and her instructions about returning the silver. He was so eager for the countess's good will that he sent her three original letters and made copies for Benjamin Franklin, the Marine Committee, and others.

The countess never replied. Her husband wrote Jones a letter venting his rage over the theft and kidnapping plan. Selkirk said taking him prisoner would have been pointless. He had no friends at King George III's court to pay his ransom, and he lacked any influence to arrange a prisoner exchange. He also wrote that Jones had been wrong to consider him an enemy. In fact, Selkirk disapproved of the way Great Britain's ministers were conducting "the unhappy and ill-judged American War."[4] Jones never received the earlier letter.

Lieutenant Simpson

Jones turned his attention to Lieutenant Thomas Simpson. Navy regulations required that an officer charged with disobeying orders must have a chance to clear himself in a military trial, or court-martial. The judges had to be three senior naval officers. There was not one in France at the time, so the case had to be postponed.

Simpson lived comfortably aboard *Ranger*, busily undermining the crew's discipline. Jones's charges omitted Simpson's efforts to incite the men to mutiny, and Lieutenant Meijer's warning before the Whitehaven raid. Miejer told Jones that Simpson had urged the men to leave Jones behind at the harbor, to be captured by the British.

Jones grew tired of Simpson's meddling. He sent the lieutenant to a French prison ship in the bay. Simpson caused so much trouble there that Jones's close friend in the French Navy, Admiral Louis Guillouet, moved him to a naval prison ashore. Many in *Ranger*'s crew defended Simpson. They were New Englanders who disliked the "outsider," Jones.

The American commissioners received plenty of mail about Simpson and other navy matters. On May 16, twenty-seven men wrote to defend Simpson's response to Jones's orders about *Drake*.[5] On June 3, Lieutenant Hall, Master Cullam, and Dr. Ezra Green wrote to request that Simpson be given a quick trial. They also asked that the prizes they had captured be sold promptly because their shares of the money were needed for their families at home.[6] Also on June 3, seventy-seven enlisted men wrote to complain of being away from home longer than the one year they had agreed to when they joined *Ranger*.[7] On June 15, another twenty-eight senior enlisted men and three officers wrote about this issue.[8]

The commissioners were increasingly impatient with complaints about Jones, and they urged him to be less severe with Simpson. They applied pressure

until he finally gave Simpson a parole, although he canceled it five weeks later. To be rid of Simpson, Jones agreed to release him to take *Ranger* back to America. The official explanation stated that the lieutenant was the only experienced navigator available.

After Simpson was released, he boasted about his assignment and publicly slandered Jones, who demanded a court-martial. Again, three senior officers could not be found. Jones's naval superiors ordered him to drop the case.

Despite his problems with Simpson, Jones made sure that *Ranger*'s crew received all the rewards due to it. These included advance money for the ship's prizes and an extra bonus for the Whitehaven landing party.

Jones Is Stranded

Jones had released *Ranger* willingly because he expected to receive another command soon. He wanted to erase what he considered the blot on his reputation made by the Simpson matter. He worried that it overshadowed his successes at Whitehaven, Saint Mary's Isle, and with *Drake*.

Possibilities for command came and went. Other captains received priority. Jones wrote to everyone he knew, and even to some he did not know, protesting his five months of idleness. Jones received no encouragement from Congress or the Marine Committee.

He moved to Paris to pursue *L'Indien* when it was mentioned again, but the ship was given to the small, private South Carolina state navy. The wealthy

Monsieur Jacques Le Ray de Chaumont offered Jones command of his privateer. Jones refused. Monsieur Gabrielle de Sartine, minister of marine, then suggested a French ship. Jones declined. He persuaded Sartine to ask Benjamin Franklin to order him to stay in France and wait for a new command.

By midsummer 1778, the British had control of almost all American coastal waters from New York north to Nova Scotia. The Continental Navy lost fifteen warships that year to capture, explosion, fire, and scuttling to avoid capture. Seven frigates and *Providence* were the only available warships. The French, as America's allies, pursued British ships near their own home ports. France kept Great Britain from succeeding in its plan to destroy all American seaports from Maine to South Carolina.

Jones was in anguish over his inability to seize enemy ships and send their cargoes to America. Franklin begged him to calm down, but Jones was out of patience. His time and talents were being left untapped, his

This engraving is made from a miniature at the Naval Lyceum, Brooklyn. It shows Captain Jones wearing a fashionable powdered wig during a visit to Paris.

skills and courage wasted. He became so difficult that his friends suggested he go home. He took offense when the commissioners had little time or patience for his troubles. He ignored their enormous diplomatic and financial burdens, long days, and lines of visitors who petitioned for every cause.

Although Jones spoke fluent French, he employed a bilingual secretary. He kept Lieutenant Peter Amiel busy writing to anyone who might solve Jones's problems. Chaumont offered a choice of several British prizes. Jones declined again. His frustration boiled over, as he declared, "I wish to have no Connection with any ship that does not sail fast, for I intend to go in harm's way."[9]

Duc de Duras

In December 1778, Jones inspected several ships at Lorient. He toured *Duc de Duras*, a thirteen-year-old merchant vessel, and found it the only available vessel to meet his

Benjamin Franklin was an American commissioner for several years. He and Jones became good friends as Franklin helped Jones professionally and socially.

requirements. He urged Chaumont to buy and arm the ship before someone else claimed it.

In February 1779, King Louis XVI of France approved the purchase of the ship in recognition of Jones's distinguished service on behalf of the United States. France owned *Duc de Duras*, and the king authorized Jones to fly the Stars and Stripes. Louis XVI paid all wages and expenses to prepare the ship. Jones enlisted an American crew and agreed to hire French crewmen when necessary to complete the roster. The French Navy directed him to leave when he was ready and to sail anywhere he chose in European or American waters.

7

BONHOMME RICHARD

Jones renamed *Duc de Duras* to honor Benjamin Franklin and his highly popular booklet, *Poor Richard's Almanac*. Translated from English to French, the book title became *Les Maximes du Bonhomme Richard*.

Richard's renovation took over six months. Jones traveled through France seeking materials and equipment. Time was short, and when a cannon manufacturer missed his deadline, Jones had to settle for used weapons with older barrels.

Bonhomme Richard carried a crew of 380 officers, men, and boys from eleven countries.[1] They rebuilt the midsection of *Richard*'s lower deck to house six additional cannons that shot eighteen-pound balls.

> **Poor Richard's Almanac**
> *Poor Richard* began in 1733 with twenty-four pages of other writers' verses, jokes, and astrological predictions for the following year. In 1746, it grew to thirty-six pages when Franklin began publishing his own writings on religion and politics. He filled blank spots on the pages with wise sayings called proverbs.

They cut gunports in the hull near the waterline. *Richard*'s arsenal expanded to forty guns.[2]

Jones and the American commissioners organized a naval squadron that included America's *Alliance*, commanded by French Navy Captain Pierre Landais. France provided *Pallas*, *Vengeance*, and *Le Cerf*, all commanded by French captains holding commissions in both the French Navy and the American Navy. As the squadron's senior captain, Jones used the courtesy title of commodore.

French and Spanish Plot

The French and Spanish governments had a secret plan. It called for Jones's squadron to attack England's west coast while France and Spain invaded from the east. Great Britain's naval forces would be divided and vulnerable. As an American ally, the French wanted to punish Great Britain for attacking America's coastal towns. Benjamin Franklin told a member of the British Parliament, "You . . . burn our towns and murder our

people. Look upon your hands! They are stained with the blood of your relations! You and I were long friends. You are now my enemy and I am yours."[3]

The young French nobleman Marquis de Lafayette sailed from America to France aboard *Alliance* to join the invasion. He was to command the landing force attached to Jones's squadron. This included fifteen hundred men, a group of soldiers on horseback, and many battlefield weapons.[4] Franklin's orders stated clearly that Lafayette would be in charge ashore, while Jones would give the orders at sea.

France canceled the attack on Great Britain in late summer because of storms in the English Channel, an epidemic of the intestinal disease typhoid fever, and various disagreements with Spain. One French officer noted that Spanish ships, "sail so badly . . . they can neither overtake an enemy nor escape from one."[5]

Marquis de Lafayette

Twenty-year-old French aristocrat Marquis de Lafayette sailed to America in 1777. Congress made him an army major general, without pay, on General Washington's staff. He and Washington became close friends. Lafayette fought in several battles and wintered with Washington's troops at Valley Forge, Pennsylvania, during 1777–1778. Lafayette went home when France declared war on England in 1779, though he later returned to help the Americans fight the British at Yorktown in 1781.

The French nobleman Marquis de Lafayette came to America to help
fight the revolution. He and Jones became friends while planning an
invasion of England that never took place.

Richard's Summer Cruise

Jones persuaded France to keep the squadron together even without an assignment. Franklin and Sartine, France's minister of marine, rescued Jones with orders for a commerce-raiding cruise. Jones was to sail past Ireland's rugged west coast, east through the Orkney Islands, and south along Great Britain's east coast. The voyage would end at the Texel, a sheltered deep-water harbor seventy-five miles from Amsterdam, Holland.

Jones had hoped for a battle and he went to see Franklin. As always, he forgot to consider the busy commissioner's many responsibilities. Franklin reminded him firmly that, because the French paid the bills, they had every right to give the orders. Franklin urged against appealing to Sartine because "there is not now time to obtain a Reconsideration."[6] He said Sartine wanted the cruise to end in the Texel because *L'Indien* was blockaded there, and might need an escort to France. Jones interpreted this news as another chance to gain command of the ship.

Troubles Begin

Jones's orders from Sartine were for "distressing the Enemies of the United States."[7] The squadron set sail on August 14, 1779. Jones's first clash with Captain Landais of *Alliance* came on August 23. The winds had died the day before, causing *Richard* to drift near the Irish coastline. Jones sent a rowing party to tow it away from the rocks. The men cut the towline and sailed away with Jones's boat. Five other crewmen left *Richard* without permission to pursue the thieves.

They became lost in a sudden fog and did not answer *Richard*'s signal guns.

Landais came aboard *Richard* the following evening, August 23, to berate Jones for sending boats and men to take a prize. He was wrong about why they went out. Nevertheless, Landais announced that he would do whatever he wanted henceforth, including "chasing when and where he thought proper and in every other matter that concerned the service."[8]

Jones had other problems. A powerful wind damaged *Le Cerf*'s main mast, forcing it to return to Lorient for repairs. *Pallas* left briefly for rudder repairs. *Richard* and *Vengeance* sailed alone. *Alliance* returned from hunting for prizes on September 1. *Pallas* returned the next day. *Alliance* left again on September 3, seeking more prizes. Jones had trouble keeping track of the squadron's comings and goings.

In mid-September, Jones signaled the captains of *Pallas* and *Vengeance* to come aboard his flagship. He showed them a map of the Firth of Forth and suggested that they raid the Scottish town of Leith. He wanted to enhance his fierce reputation by alarming the citizens. The other captains refused. They became much more interested when Jones mentioned a two-hundred-thousand-pound ransom the Leith town council might pay him to go away. However, the plan failed even before it began. A powerful storm blew *Richard* down the firth and out to sea.

The squadron did not go unnoticed. Sentries at Edinburgh's fortress spotted the ships, inspiring rumors in both Edinburgh and Leith that "Jones the

Pirate" was near. Bugles called militiamen to duty while ministers prayed for the people's protection. Citizens hid their valuables, grabbed their children, locked their doors, and ran away. The hysteria continued long after *Richard* sailed away.

The squadron caught the merchant ship *Union*, which carried a cargo of winter uniforms for the British Army in Canada. Jones sent the uniforms to America immediately. The cruise had produced few good prizes. Jones scuttled every ship he did not consider valuable. He regretted that, after five weeks at sea, the crew did not have any exciting memories of raids, ransoms, invasions, or victories. *Ranger* would be leaving for the Texel in Holland the following week. The squadron was to escort a fleet of French merchant ships transporting naval supplies from the Baltic Sea to Brest, France.

Richard and *Serapis*

On September 23, *Richard*, *Alliance*, *Pallas*, and *Vengeance* cruised near Flamborough Head on England's Yorkshire coast. Jones knew that a fleet of forty-one British merchant ships was due any day. If he captured them, *Richard*'s crew would receive plenty of prize money to make up for their lack of prizes so far.

Captain Richard Pearson of Britain's Royal Navy neared Flamborough Head about noon after crossing the North Sea with a merchant fleet. Pearson's H.M.S. *Serapis* was a new fifty-gun, copper-bottomed vessel. It was escorted by Captain Thomas Piercy's

Countess of Scarborough. Pearson noticed red warning flags ashore, and a boatman from town confirmed John Paul Jones's presence south of Flamborough Head. Pearson signaled the merchant ships to head for Scarborough Castle.

Pearson rounded Flamborough Head at one o'clock and spotted four ships in the distance, all flying British flags. He recognized Jones's trick of using an enemy's flag to get close enough to attack. Aboard *Richard*, the lookout spotted *Serapis*. Jones ordered his helmsman, Samuel Stacey, to change course and head north.

Ten miles of open ocean separated the gliding warships. *Serapis* was new, sleek, fast, and heavily armed. *Richard* was old, bulky, slow, and had fewer guns. Both vessels buzzed with battle preparations.

Serapis and *Countess of Scarborough* would have been outnumbered and outgunned if Jones had fought in the usual manner. Pearson expected him to form a line of battle and fire cannons as his squadron passed the British warships. Pearson's chances soared when Jones signaled the squadron to stand together. But, they did not. *Alliance* turned away, *Pallas* followed, and *Vengeance* wandered, leaving *Richard* to fight alone.

Engagement

Pearson hailed for *Richard*'s identity. Helmsman Stacey answered, "The Royal Princess."[9] When he was asked again, his response was lost in blasts fired from both ships. *Serapis*'s broadside killed several men and tore through *Richard*'s hull at the waterline. A

carpenter quickly plugged the holes with wooden pegs covered with sticky fibers.

Jones's recently acquired guns misfired and exploded, killing several men, destroying the gun site, and setting fire to the deck above. Suddenly, he had only twelve reliable cannons. *Serapis*'s gunfire targeted *Richard*'s sails and the French Marines high above the deck. Jones later said, the "fire of their cannon was incessant."[10] He knew *Serapis* could win the battle just by staying a few hundred feet away and bombarding *Richard*. The Americans' best chance was hand-to-hand combat. Jones ordered his men to lob grenades at sharpshooters on *Serapis*'s deck and prepare to go aboard as soon as an opportunity came.

Serapis's guns blazed as the ship crossed in front of *Richard*. The British ship turned slowly, allowing *Richard*'s bow to ram it from behind. Against thundering muskets and cannons, British Captain Pearson

The Watchers

The battle between *Bonhomme Richard* and *Serapis* began at sundown and raged under a bright full moon. A thousand Irish spectators came to watch the cornered pirate—Jones—meet his end. They could see flames shooting up the riggings and sails catching fire high aloft on both ships. They could not see blood darkening the wooden decks. Nor could they hear the moans and cries of dying men.

During the battle between the Bonhomme Richard *and the* Serapis, *John Paul Jones refused to surrender, yelling, "I have not yet begun to fight."*

called to ask if Jones would surrender. Jones raised his sword and yelled, "I have not yet begun to fight."[11]

Jones needed a better angle for an attack, but his men were busy putting out fires. A slight breeze edged *Richard* close to *Serapis*'s bow and blocked the wind in its sail. *Serapis* slowed and tangled its bow in *Richard*'s rigging. Jones's men grabbed clawlike grappling hooks and thick ropes to lash the ships tightly. The two vessels pivoted together, keeping the heavily damaged *Richard* afloat. Richard's men jumped aboard *Serapis* to fight amid flames and smoke. Jones

Moonlight illuminated the fury of battle near Flamborough Head between Bonhomme Richard *and* Serapis. *The painting is by Thomas Mitchell, done in 1780.*

saw, "Ships were Set on fire in Various places . . . the Scene was dreadful."[12]

The American ship *Alliance* returned at 9:30 P.M. Ignoring Jones's frantic distress signals, it passed the bound ships several times, firing broadsides into *Richard* and killing many men. Jones could not believe it. A crewman asked why he did not give up. Jones refused to lower his flag. He said, "No, I will sink, I will never strike."[13]

William Hamilton, a Scottish volunteer aboard *Richard*, crawled onto a horizontal pole called a yardarm high above the deck. He carried a bucket of grenades to hurl down onto *Serapis*'s deck. One wobbled through an open hatch and blew up the British ship's lower gun deck. The explosion rocked both vessels, further damaging *Richard*'s hull and killing twenty men.

Richard was now ablaze from end to end. One whole side was gone. Sailors raced to free dozens of prisoners who were trapped below deck and terrified of drowning. Lieutenant Richard Dale put them to working the pumps to keep *Richard* afloat.

Jones and his wounded gunnery officer dragged a cannon across the deck and aimed it at *Serapis*'s mainmast. Jones realized that, if the mast came down, taking *Serapis*'s sails along with it, Pearson would have to surrender. While *Richard*'s officers urged Jones to give up, the gun crew shot away the last of *Serapis*'s mainmast. The sails, riggings, and sail supports toppled into the sea.

Pearson surrendered. At 10:30, Lieutenant Dale boarded *Serapis* to escort Pearson to *Richard*. The British captain handed his sword to Jones, who returned it at once out of respect for a worthy adversary. Jones then invited Pearson to his cabin for a glass of wine.

The Battle of Flamborough Head lasted more than three hours. The conflict cost each side nearly half its crew. *Serapis* was in terrible condition. *Richard* was in even worse shape. It had sustained severe damage, including the attacks by *Alliance*. Jones also lost the prize money he would have won by capturing the merchant fleet.

Dr. Lawrence Brooke and his aides attended the wounded while the dead were buried at sea with full

military honors. The crew rigged bits of *Serapis*'s sail and tied ropes to *Richard*, hoping to tow the ship to a friendly port. Crewmen patched holes and pumped water, but they could not prevail against the invading sea. *Richard* was low in the water as the squadron moved slowly east.

After thirty-six hours, Jones knew there was no hope. He gave orders to abandon ship. Hundreds of wounded men were transferred to the squadron's other vessels. Through the morning of September 25, *Richard* wallowed in the swells, tattered sails set, its

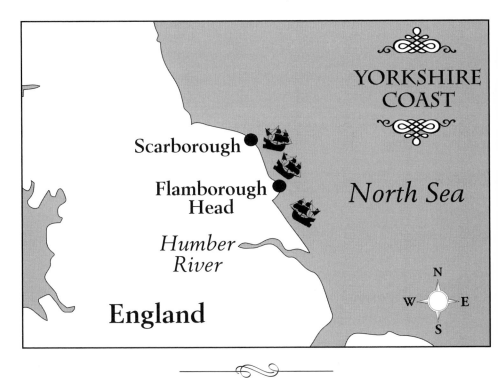

After Alliance, Pallas, *and* Vengeance *left* Bonhomme Richard *alone, the ship sailed north to face* Serapis, *which was escorted by* Countess of Scarborough.

American flag still fluttering in the breeze. The former *Duc de Duras* had been through a lot since King Louis XVI of France gave Jones command of it. When the *Bonhomme Richard* could no longer stay afloat, the gallant ship nosed forward, slipped silently beneath the waves, and was gone.

8

THE TEXEL
AND BEYOND

News of the battle's stunning outcome traveled
fast throughout Great Britain, causing greater
chaos than the Whitehaven raid and *Drake*'s capture.
People talked of little else but Jones. His reputation
soared. People imagined they saw him everywhere.

Newspapers opposed to Britain's policies used
Jones as a weapon to annoy the government. They
touted him as "a pirate indeed, a plunderer, but . . .
not a Barbarian."[1] Publishers printed cheap paperback
books about England's latest Robin Hood.

Newspapers that supported the British government investigated Jones's childhood and interviewed
his crewmen. The London *Morning Post* wrote that he
popped up and then vanished, "to mislead our Marines

London newspapers fanned the fears of British subjects about "Pirate Jones" and pictured him in many absurd settings. This image shows his costume decorated with a "skull and crossbones" emblem.

and terrify our coasts . . . he is no sooner seen than lost."[2]

Other countries also followed Jones's escapades. The French loved the uproar over America's "pirate." They appreciated his way of keeping the British off balance by dividing their ships and resources. It helped give France the freedom to challenge Great Britain for control of the seas and the rich West Indies trade.

General George Washington regarded Jones's impact as evidence that navies, not armies, would decide the outcome of the American Revolution. He believed only "if we had the command of the seas" could his army and its allies undertake strong, coordinated campaigns.[3]

Politics in Holland

Jones escaped by an indirect route after evading the ships searching for him. A British Navy ship met a Dutch merchant vessel on October 10 and learned that Jones had arrived at the Texel the previous week aboard the damaged *Serapis*. He was accompanied by *Alliance*, *Pallas*, *Vengeance*, and *Countess of Scarborough*. Jones wanted to use a French port, but the other captains followed Sartine's orders to end the cruise at the Texel. Five British warships arrived within weeks to blockade them at their dock.

Richard's officers and men had plenty of company in port. The Dutch showered them with gifts and attention. Jones wrote to Commissioner John Adams in Paris: "Every day the blessed women come to the ships in great numbers . . . bringing . . . for our

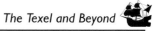

wounded . . . comforts of Dutch homes . . . from the hearts of the people . . ."[4] The children had a favorite song about Jones and every stanza began, "Here comes Paul Jones; such a nice man!"[5]

Jones reported to the American commissioners that the Dutch were politically neutral in the war because they were making a fortune handling most of Europe's shipping business. He said his greatest satisfaction came from using his situation to cause serious problems between Holland and England.

Europe's high councils debated the complex problems related to Jones. Meanwhile, he attended to over five hundred prisoners, many of them wounded. He worked to resolve the delicate political issue of American soldiers guarding British prisoners on neutral Dutch soil. After many appeals, Jones received permission to move the injured men, guarded by French Marines, to a fort on Texel Island. A prominent and wealthy Dutch businessman helped him obtain food, water, and approval to repair his ships.

Jones had less success with healthy prisoners. He offered to release British officers and frequently asked to exchange British prisoners for jailed Americans. Captain Pearson refused, fearing that, in his absence, his leaderless crew would join the United States Navy.

Great Britain's ambassador to Holland, Sir Joseph Yorke, considered having Jones arrested, but there was no evidence of a crime. He pressured the Dutch to force Jones to surrender the squadron and leave. The Dutch government, in a tight vote, decided that Jones had to go and ordered him to leave the Texel. The

An American Prisoner

Jones wanted to exchange British Captain Pearson for Gustavus Conyngham, an American Jones had never met. As captain of the Continental cutter *Revenge*, Conyngham captured a stunning sixty prizes in eighteen months before going to England's infamous Mill Prison. He dug his way out and escaped in November 1779. Jones welcomed him to *Alliance* and invited him to stay until he received a new command.

French ambassador convinced Jones that *Vengeance, Pallas, Serapis,* and *Scarborough* must become France's responsibilities and fly French flags. *Serapis* and *Pallas* remained in port when *Vengeance* and *Scarborough* departed to take nearly two hundred British prisoners back to Great Britain.

Commissioner Benjamin Franklin ordered Captain Landais to Paris to explain why he deliberately fired on *Richard* during the Battle of Flamborough Head. Landais left *Alliance* in terrible condition, with disorderly officers and a sickly crew. It took Jones and his men weeks to clean and refit the ship. He used every tactic he knew to stall the squadron's departure from Holland until *Alliance* was ready to sail. The Dutch government was becoming impatient with the political turmoil surrounding him.

Alliance Returns to France

Alliance could not leave the Texel without sailing into British warships waiting nearby. Winter arrived with howling winds and heavy sleet. Jones watched for the right moment to make his move.

It came in the early morning of December 27, 1779. A gale churned the sea, blowing the British blockade temporarily off station. With *Alliance*'s guns ready, Jones hoisted the Stars and Stripes, slipped the ship's cables, and left the harbor.

Alliance raced by the amazed harbor master and the British warships, down the North Sea to the English Channel. It sped past an English fleet at Spithead and the town of Plymouth into the North Atlantic. It logged seventy miles in seven hours of flying with the wind.[6]

Jones cruised for several weeks, happy to be at sea. The crew grumbled because he did not go directly to France. He kept them busy rearranging *Alliance*'s interior layout, guided by tradesmen and craftsmen he borrowed from other ships. The ship reached Lorient, France, on February 19, 1780.

Franklin wrote to Jones the same day, asking him to transport an enormous cargo to General Washington's army. It included sixteen thousand weapons from Lafayette, and one hundred twenty bales of uniform cloth.[7] Jones also had to carry passengers. Among them was Arthur Lee, a former commissioner, who disliked Franklin and Jones. Lee insisted on taking a mountain of baggage, including his

traveling coach. Warships had little storage space and Jones refused his demands.

Alliance's crew was unhappy about the lack of prize money. Monsieur Chaumont, who was responsible for selling prizes and distributing the cash, kept postponing the sales. Sartine, the minister of marine, wanted to buy *Serapis* and *Countess of Scarborough* for a specific amount of money per cannon. *Alliance*'s officers and men insisted that an auction would be more profitable. They were wrong. It made less money than a price-per-gun sale would have brought. Jones went to Paris in April to resolve the matter, leaving *Alliance* idle for weeks.

Jones in Paris

The trip was a special time in Jones's life. The city of Paris welcomed Jones as a conquering hero. Commissioner John Adams described "the Clamor of Paris . . . in . . . favour of . . . Jones . . . and the inclination of the Ladies to embrace him . . ."[8] The captain was the guest of honor at magnificent parties, where he renewed friendships with powerful and influential people. Beautiful women flirted with him, and he eagerly returned their attentions. He wrote long letters to friends about his exciting social life and his favorite lady of the moment.

Franklin introduced Jones to fellow Masons who invited him to join France's distinguished Lodge of the Nine Sisters. They engaged the renowned sculptor Jean-Antoine Houdon to carve his likeness in a marble bust. The trip's highlight came when King Louis XVI

of France indicated his desire to grant Jones France's Order of Military Merit. Because no foreign officer may accept a royal tribute without his government's approval, Sartine wrote to Congress for permission on the King's behalf.

Jones's excitement in Paris ended abruptly. On June 1, he finally received Benjamin Franklin's letter ordering him back to *Alliance*. He left quickly but stopped for a week in Nantes, France, to visit Masons he had known during his *Ranger* days. He arrived in Lorient in mid-June and reported to the crew that the French government had not decided about selling prizes. Therefore, he could not yet obtain their money. Jones said he had urged Sartine to sell the ships and pressured Chaumont to release the crew's money, but both refused.

Jones was exasper-ated to find General Washington's shipment and Arthur Lee's cargo still waiting on the dock. *Alliance* was full, and Jones needed another ship. Franklin had no

French sculptor Antoine Houdon created a life-size marble bust of Jones in 1780. He used Jones's exact measurements and proportions. The captain ordered copies made as gifts.

money to charter one. Jones suggested a naval vessel, and Minister Sartine authorized the *Ariel*. It was too small. Jones still needed more space.

Landais Again

Jones's return to Lorient was badly timed. Pierre Landais, former captain of *Alliance*, was en route to America for his court-martial. He had not been able to convince Franklin that his rounds of fire on *Richard* were mistakes. Landais and a newfound friend, Arthur Lee, were plotting to reclaim *Alliance*. They convinced the surly crew that Jones had not protected their financial interests. Landais persuaded 115 officers and men to sign a complaint about Jones, demanding back pay, prize money, and Landais's return to command *Alliance*.[9]

Franklin wrote to Jones about the mutinous plot, but his letter arrived too late. Franklin wrote to Landais, warning him to stop scheming for command of his old ship. He cautioned Jones's crew to support their current captain. Jones did not realize the extent of the problem until Landais revealed his intentions on June 12. He claimed command of *Alliance* and ordered everyone ashore who had served on *Richard*.

Jones promptly left for Paris to protest Landais's actions. Although Sartine supported him, he believed Jones should have stayed in Lorient. When Jones returned on June 20, Washington's weapons and uniform cloth were still sitting on the dock. Arthur Lee and his belongings were safely aboard the departing *Alliance*.

Jones wrote a hasty note to Monsieur Antoine Thévenard, captain of the port, telling him to stop *Alliance* before it reached open sea. Jones and Thévenard, who monitored Lorient's shipping traffic, had a deal to halt Landais if he tried to leave without permission. Jones changed his mind and canceled the agreement because *Alliance*'s departure would rid him of both Landais and Lee.

Ariel in Lorient

Ariel arrived in Lorient during the *Alliance* turmoil, on loan from the French Navy to help solve Franklin's problem. Jones changed its sails and waited for a second ship, which did not come. Franklin could not send one. It was increasingly expensive to charter ships because the value of Continental money was declining. It took increasing amounts of American cash to exchange for equal value in European money.

Meanwhile, Washington's cargo had grown by hundreds more barrels of gunpowder and ten thousand military uniforms. Jones reduced *Ariel*'s weapons and crew by half to make room for half the cargo. He pleaded for two merchant ships and Franklin finally found them. On July 18, the crew started loading. *Ariel* was ready by August 25, but Jones stayed in Lorient two more weeks. After leaving, he was detained for a month at Groix Roads, France, due to bad weather. On October 7, *Ariel* left for America with two merchant ships *Luke* and *Duke of Leinster*.

The weather was terrible. Jones wrote that he had never imagined "the awful Majesty of Tempest & of

ship Wreak."[10] *Ariel*, low in the water with a heavy load, bounced like a cork in the roiling sea. Gale winds blew the ship toward the rocks. Jones ordered the crew to cut away sections of the masts to control it. The main mast crashed onto the deck, destroying another mast, sails, decks, and hardware.

Ariel tossed for two days and nights before the storm subsided. Jones passed the wreckage-strewn coastline as his ship limped back to port using a temporary sail. Jones's seamanship won great praise when *Ariel* sailed slowly into port backward, stern first. The captain of the port wrote to Monsieur Sartine, praising Jones for saving the ship.

Ariel's repairs took two months. Jones wrote many unsuccessful letters seeking another vessel to carry General Washington's cargo. He finally sailed again on December 18, taking a long southern route with milder weather. Jones reached Philadelphia on February 18, 1781. Three years and three months had passed since he sailed from America aboard *Ranger*. He planned to pursue the reimbursements and back pay owed to him for years.

AFTER THE REVOLUTION

Congress began hearings for Landais's court-martial in February 1781, before *Ariel* reached Philadelphia. Upon his arrival Jones was ordered to appear before the Navy's Board of Admiralty, the office in charge of naval affairs, about General Washington's cargo. He received forty-seven questions concerning its management, to be answered in writing.

Jones brought to America letters of praise from Franklin, Lafayette, and two French ministers of marine. He carried Sartine's request that Louis XVI be allowed to give Jones special awards. Jones's documents impressed Congress so much that it passed a resolution on February 27 honoring his bravery and military conduct and called his seamanship at the

 John Paul Jones

Battle of Flamborough Head "so brilliant as to excite
. . . applause and admiration."[1]

Jones became the first American to receive
France's Order of Military Merit. The honor was
reserved for Protestant foreign officers serving in
France, a largely Roman Catholic country. Philadelphia
society joined Congress to see the French ambassador,
Minister Chevalier de la Luzerne, pin the gold cross
and ribbon on Jones's uniform. Congress asked
Franklin to inform King Louis XVI of its appreciation.
The award entitled Jones to call himself Chevalier, or
Sir, for life. Louis also had authorized another, greater
honor. Jones received a gold-hilt sword with the
inscription, "Louis XVI rewards the Stout Vindicator
of the Freedom of the Seas."[2]

On March 21, 1781, Jones submitted his answers
about Washington's cargo to the Board of Admiralty.
The board decided the mistakes and confusion were
caused by weather, lack of money, and Landais's bad
conduct. It recommended that Congress recognize
Jones's concern for the "officers and men who have
faithfully served under him."[3]

On May 19, General Washington wrote to Jones
about Louis XVI's tribute and the victory at
Flamborough Head. He said these could only be
earned through "long and honorable service, or . . .
brilliant action."[4] The letter remained among Jones's
most treasured possessions.

This engraving of John Paul Jones is by J. B. Longacre, from a portrait by Charles Willson Peale. Jones wears his medal for the Order of Military Merit, bestowed by French King Louis XVI.

Status of the Navy

The navy had changed during six years of warfare. Most of its original ships had been captured, sold, sunk, blockaded, or idled for lack of a crew. No new ships were scheduled as Jones looked for a command. He contacted Robert Morris, the new agent of marine, whose office replaced the Board of Admiralty. The seventy-four-gun *America*, approved years earlier, was not yet completed. Morris offered and Jones accepted its command, hoping this would lead to a new fleet. He still aspired to the senior rank of rear admiral.

During his life, Jones received medals from the French Order of Military Merit, the Society of Cincinnati, and the Russian Order of St. Anne. After his death, he was awarded a medal from the Military and Hospitaller Order of St. Lazarus of Jerusalem.

The End of the Revolutionary War
Most of the fighting of the revolution ended in America following General Washington's victory over British General Charles Cornwallis at Yorktown, Virginia, in October 1781. Negotiations for peace took place, while occasional small battles were still fought. In 1783, the United States and Great Britain signed the Treaty of Paris, which finally ended the war in favor of the new and independent United States.

Jones spent several months untangling his finances. He had lived on his savings and prize money during the war because the navy did not pay him for six years. He needed reimbursement for loans to his crews and the many expenses he covered for *Alfred, Ranger,* and *Providence.* After waiting for months, Jones collected $20,705.27 in cash on December 9, 1782.[5] He gave it to his friend John Ross to invest for him.

Jones arrived in Portsmouth, New Hampshire, at the end of August 1782 to supervise *America*'s completion. He lodged with Widow Purcell again and rejoined the town's social life. No longer considered an outsider, he received a hero's welcome.

America was the largest ship to be built in Portsmouth. It was farther behind schedule than Jones expected. John Langdon, *Ranger*'s builder, had started and stopped construction for three years. He and Jones resumed their animosity and rarely spoke. They communicated through Robert Morris and his

secretary, John Brown, in Philadelphia. Jones met with Brown in secret, out of Langdon's hearing.

In July 1782, a French fleet of sixteen ships commanded by Lieutenant General Marquis de Vaudreuil entered Boston Harbor. *Le Magnifique* hit a submerged rock at high tide and broke apart as the tide went out. Its cannons and fittings were given to *America*. Congress saw a solution to the expensive dilemma of *America* and gave the ship to King Louis XVI. It replaced *Le Magnifique* and signified the country's gratitude for France's participation in the war.

America was launched on November 12, 1782, with French and American flags flying from the stern. Under Jones's careful guidance, it missed rocks along Portsmouth's Piscataqua River and eased into the new dock. Jones transferred *America* to Capitaine de Vaisseau de Macarty-Macteigne, former captain of *Le Magnifique*, who accepted it into France's Royal Navy.

A Caribbean Cruise

Jones left Portsmouth for Philadelphia in November 1782, seeking another command. He could not refuse an opportunity that came his way in December. Marquis de Vaudreuil invited him to cruise to the Caribbean aboard his flagship, *Le Triomphant*. They sailed on Christmas Eve to join a second French fleet and a Spanish fleet in the harbor at Puerto Cabello, Venezuela.

The weather was hot and humid. Mosquitoes thrived in the bushy mangrove trees surrounding the harbor. Their bites spread illnesses such as malaria and yellow fever. Jones was fine when Vaudreuil's fleet sailed for America on April 8, 1783. However, after arriving in Philadelphia in mid-May, he became ill and spent months in a Pennsylvania hospital.

Jones had sailed with Vaudreuil to study battle tactics and how naval fleets developed through history. Far from real battles, more than one hundred well-educated, experienced officers discussed and debated ancient wars. They returned to reality when a passing frigate reported the signing of a peace treaty in Paris on April 1, 1783, to end the Revolutionary War. Fighting in American waters ended on April 7.

The change was good for America but not for its navy. Jones wrote to Robert Morris and Congress about the need to establish a permanent force of trained naval officers. He knew first-hand that young men needed solid experience to prepare for leadership. He told Congress, "In time of Peace, it is necessary to prepare, and be *always prepared*, for War by Sea."[6]

Quest for Prize Money

Morris accepted Jones's suggestion that he go to Europe and collect prize money long overdue to the crews of *Alliance*, *Ranger*, and *Bonhomme Richard*. Congress agreed on November 1, 1783, and authorized an agent's fee for him. Jones left in December 1783, after joining other Continental Army and Navy officers to establish the Society of the Cincinnati with George Washington as the first president.

Jones met with Franklin in Paris. The commissioner wrote a personal note authorizing him to work on behalf of those who had served in his commands. Jones renewed friendships with the Masons. He was presented again to King Louis XVI on December 20. The King told Jones he would always be available to help him.

In early 1786, Jones presented to Louis a detailed book in French about his life from 1775 through 1784. He kept a copy for himself. The *Memoire* was a reminder of his desire to become an admiral in the French Navy. War between France and Spain loomed briefly, but it faded along with his hope for flag rank.

Jones spent two years pursuing prize money, although he knew where it was all the time. Monsieur Le Ray de Chaumont kept *Richard*'s money, claiming it as reimbursement for outfitting the ship. He and

Jones argued over details about the cost of this and who should pay for that.

After settling their differences, Jones waited another year for the

Thomas Jefferson and John Paul Jones became friends when Jefferson replaced Benjamin Franklin as American commissioner in Paris. They worked together to resolve the issue of prize money.

money. He became reacquainted with Thomas Jefferson, whom he had met through Dr. John Read years earlier in Philadelphia. Jefferson replaced Franklin as the only American minister handling American affairs in France.

While waiting for Chaumont, Jones traveled to Lorient, France, to collect money for *Alliance*'s crew. Another agent, Monsieur Puchilberg, claimed sole authority over the funds. Jones wrote to Jefferson many times, asking for resolution. On August 5, 1786, Jefferson and Jones agreed on the final amounts for back pay and reimbursements. Jones won $22,435 for the crews and $13,560 for himself.[7]

Jones went to New York the following year, where Congress voted him a gold commemorative medal. Jefferson was instructed to have it made in Paris by the leading artist, Augustin Dupré, and to inform King Louis XVI of the honor.

Russia

Jones learned that Russian Empress Catherine II knew of him through several sources. She

Congress authorized a gold medal to honor Jones in October 1787. Augustin Dupré, an artist in Paris, used Houdon's bust as his model for the profile. The Bonhomme Richard *and* Serapis *battle is on the other side.*

Catherine the Great

Catherine II was a German princess who married Peter, heir to the Russian throne. When he became emperor in 1762, she gained great influence. Eventually, she took the throne for herself. An intellectual woman, she opened schools and hospitals, supported the arts, and encouraged women's education. She favored the upper class, however, and did little for the common people.

wanted him to lead a naval expedition to Constantinople, Turkey. Jefferson had recommended Jones to Monsieur Simolin, Russian minister to France's Royal Court in Versailles. On February 1, 1788, Simolin met with Jones and reported to Catherine of Jones's interest in her plans.

Catherine had been expanding Russia's borders by peacefully taking over neighboring nations. In 1788, the second Russo-Turkish War was into its second year. Catherine and her enemy, the Sultan of Turkey, had clear goals. Catherine wanted the Black Sea, a gateway to the city of Constantinople, Turkey, and to the Mediterranean Sea. The sultan intended to stop her.

The Sultan had a fort at Ochakov, at the mouth of a river called the Liman. Catherine wanted to displace the Turks from the Liman and capture Ochakov. The Sultan planned to destroy her fleets and retake territory Turkey had lost in previous campaigns.

Catherine owned a fleet of mediocre ships with inexperienced, ill-trained sailors. Many of her officers were adventurers with few ties to Russia. She needed Jones's experience, and she offered the one thing he wanted. On April 15, 1788, Catherine appointed him Rear Admiral Paul-Jones of the Imperial Russian Navy.

Jones received a cordial welcome from all except twenty British officers in Russia's service. They threatened to resign rather than work with him. They were insignificant compared to Jones's greatest threat, the powerful Russian prince, Grigori Potemkin. Catherine was extremely close to Potemkin and treated him as her equal.

Potemkin wielded great power as commander in chief of Russia's armed forces. He considered Jones unnecessary because Russia already had three rear admirals in the Black Sea. Jones came with the expectation of commanding all Russian naval forces. Instead, he had one squadron, a flagship, and twelve assorted vessels.

Jones endured months of frustration, disagreement, and palace intrigue. Potemkin took credit for everything, including Catherine's success against the Turks. After an argument about planning, Jones expressed his thoughts to Potemkin in a letter and soon lost his command. While assuring Jones of his high regard, Potemkin wrote to Catherine and discussed the admiral most disrespectfully. The Russian officers in his command were the only ones loyal to him.

In late 1788, Jones left for western Russia to join Catherine's fleet at St. Petersburg on the Baltic Sea. He caught pneumonia and did not arrive for work at the navy's First Admiralty District until early

December. Jones did not speak Russian, and he was lonely when he met the French ambassador, Comte de Ségur, who became his friend. Jones waited months for Catherine to order his return for a new command. He realized by early summer that this would not happen. He asked her permission to go home.

Jones had many unhappy times in Russia, but he liked the Russian officers and crewmen. Catherine granted him a two-year leave of absence with pay and rank. He said good-bye in early July 1789, and began the long journey to France the following month.

Jones was unwell and downcast after returning to Paris. He moved to an apartment near the Masonic Lodge of the Nine Sisters. He wrote to American friends, saying he would come to visit, but he never went. His letters did not mention the French Revolution, or the uncertain fate of King Louis XVI. He only said he must stay in Paris until he could see what the political changes would bring.

Jones spent his final months hidden from a busy world, seeing a few friends and writing letters. He wrote to his sisters, who did not speak to each other, urging them to forget their differences. He also inquired about his nephews' educations. He wrote to Catherine II about military plans and future possibilities, but she did not respond.

American Citizenship

On July 10, 1790, Jones led an American delegation to celebrate the first-year anniversary of France's new constitution. In 1788, America's Congress had ratified its own new constitution, and in 1789, George Washington became the first president of the United States.

President Washington signed a petition on June 1, 1792, which was countersigned by Secretary of State Thomas Jefferson. It granted John Paul Jones American citizenship and made him an American commissioner with "full powers to negotiate . . . ransom of American Citizens in captivity . . . and sign a Convention thereupon."[8] Washington appointed Jones the American consul, or representative, to Algeria, in north Africa. Jefferson authorized a treaty and gathered money to rescue and return thirteen prisoners captured by Barbary pirates in the region.

10

EPILOGUE

Jones never knew that George Washington had granted him American citizenship. He was ill with pneumonia and alone in Paris, except for a servant, his doctor, and a few friends. Colonel Samuel Blackden, a retired colonel from North Carolina, often came to chat with him about life in the United States.

On July 18, 1792, Jones notified American Ambassador Gouverneur Morris that he was sure he was dying. When Morris arrived at his apartment, Jones was sitting in a chair, ready to dictate his will. He named Robert Morris as his executor and dictated an itemized list of his properties, including land, stocks, and cash. He left everything to his sisters, Janet Taylor and Mary Ann Lowden, in Scotland.[1]

Morris, before leaving for a dinner engagement, promised to return at eight o'clock. During his absence, Jones walked to his bedchamber, lay facedown on the bed, and died. His forty-fifth birthday had passed, unnoticed, twelve days earlier.

Monsieur Pierre-François Simonneau was the commissioner of Jones's residential district. He and Samuel Blackden planned Jones's funeral. Simonneau paid all funeral expenses himself to ensure that the famous captain received a proper burial. He also notified France's Legislative Assembly of Jones's death.

Preparation for Burial

Simonneau ordered that Jones's body be wrapped in cloth, rather than the usual military uniform with medals.[2] According to Blackden, Simonneau had the body preserved in alcohol, placed in a lead coffin, and surrounded with straw in case it should be sent to America in the future.

Jones had few special possessions other than those he left to his sisters. Simonneau auctioned his uniforms, medals, and most personal items on October 20 to settle routine bills. Louis XVI's gold sword went to his family. Remaining items included two small portraits, a pistol, and a 1777 painting of Jones's coat of arms. Simonneau also found his commission as a captain in the United States Navy and his membership in the Society of the Cincinnati.[3]

The Funeral

Presbyterian Reverend Paul-Henri Marron conducted the service two days later. French law required that Jones be buried in the only Protestant cemetery for foreigners, located outside the walls of Paris.

Mourners, led by uniformed French soldiers drumming a slow beat, walked four miles past the city gates and into the countryside. Behind them came Jones's hearse, Colonel Blackden, representatives of the Legislative Assembly in horse-drawn carriages, four members of the Presbyterian parish, Masons, and townspeople. Reverend Marron spoke of Jones's bravery and heroism. The coffin was lowered as the grenadiers fired a final round of shots.

Found Again

Jones lay in obscurity for over a century. In 1899, General Horace Porter became America's ambassador to France. Jones's history intrigued him. Since his death, the United States Navy had become the strong fighting force Jones envisioned and wanted to lead. Porter researched for years to find any record indicating that Jones was buried in Saint Louis Cemetery in Paris.[4]

Many cemeteries were lost as Paris grew. The city now covered what used to be countryside, including the one Protestant cemetery. Porter persevered until he found the right area, which had become a disreputable neighborhood. It took two years to buy properties and obtain permission to dig under the streets and buildings where the burial grounds had been. Porter's search narrowed to a site that yielded numerous coffins. Five were intact and made of lead. Three were ruled out because they bore nameplates. The fourth was meant for a tall person. The fifth one had to be Jones.

Searchers found the coffin on April 8, 1905, at Grange-aux-Belles Street, No. 43.[5] After six years, the search was over. Porter arranged for three doctors to autopsy the body at the Medical School of Practice of the Faculty of Medicine. It was moved secretly to the school, protected by Monsieur Lepine, prefect of police.

The coffin was opened on April 9. Dr. J. Capitan led the team of doctors, and he recorded every detail of the autopsy. He described the preparation for burial and agreed that it was protected for a future journey, probably to America. They measured and compared the corpse's head with Jones's bust by Houdon. Everything matched, down to the identical ear lobes.

Special Honors

A special service was held at the American Church in Paris on July 6, 1905, the anniversary of Jones's birth 158 years earlier. His coffin rested inside a large mahogany casket draped with American flags. A horse-drawn wagon bore it in a grand procession through the streets of Paris to the train station. French and American dignitaries and military representatives accompanied it.

Arriving in Cherbourg, France, the casket was piped aboard U.S.S. *Brooklyn*, flagship of a squadron

sent from America to escort the body. Three cruisers and seven battleships accompanied *Brooklyn* on the thirteen-day transatlantic crossing. The fleet entered Chesapeake Bay in single file. The first four battleships fired fifteen-gun salutes as *Brooklyn* steamed upriver toward the United States Naval Academy in Annapolis, Maryland.

Home at Last

On April 24, 1906, nearly a year after Jones's body arrived, President Theodore Roosevelt gave the eulogy at his second funeral. More than one thousand invited guests heard Roosevelt honor the officer he credited

The bronze feet of Jones's sarcophagus are shaped like dolphins, the sea creatures that have entertained seafarers for centuries.

with beginning the navy's traditions of heroism and victory. Roosevelt said, "Every officer . . . should . . . desire to emulate the energy, the professional capacity, the indomitable determination and dauntless scorn of death which marked John Paul Jones above all his fellows."[6]

The casket waited under the grand staircase in the Naval Academy's Bancroft Hall for eight years. In 1912, Congress provided funds to finish building the chapel. Jones's body was moved to the specially designed crypt below the altar on January 26, 1913.

Jones's stately marble sarcophagus (a stone coffin) rests there, on bronze feet shaped like dolphins. For centuries, these playful mammals have accompanied seafarers the world over, leaping and diving in the spray of a fast ship. John Paul Jones is sailing with the dolphins again.

Legacy

"Was it proof of madness in the first corps of sea officers . . . to have so critical a period launched out in the ocean with only two armed merchant ships, two armed brigantines and one armed sloop?" John Paul Jones asked the question after the Revolutionary War, referring to General Washington's cruisers of 1775.[7]

It was not madness. It took great courage to believe in a hastily assembled, untrained, untested navy that fought a powerful enemy in foreign waters while trying to protect its home front.

John Paul Jones is called the Father of the American Navy. Although George Washington recognized the

need for a strong naval force, Jones understood how to create one. He was not inspired by his superiors in the Continental Navy, many of whom were former merchant ship captains or political appointees. His own instincts and vision guided him.

Jones did things in his own way throughout his career. He trained crews well and set high standards of performance. He believed in a chain of command and expected orders to be obeyed without question. He took great care with his personal appearance and required the same of his officers and men.

Jones championed a permanent, well-educated, experienced officer corps. Experience taught him that

Jones was buried in the crypt below the altar at the chapel of the United States Naval Academy.

junior officers needed solid training in seamanship. He studied history and applied its lessons aboard ship. Jones's beliefs began to bear fruit when President James K. Polk established the Naval School at Annapolis in 1845. It was renamed the United States Naval Academy five years later. The academy has grown from a few small buildings to a world-class university designed to produce professional naval officers.

Going to sea in the eighteenth century was tough. Lives were at stake and there was no room for those without tenacity and courage. Jones had an abundance of both and never flinched in a tight spot. He preferred to seize the advantage by taking a fight to the enemy, a strategy that America adopted and has used for over two hundred years.

Jones's "pirate" exploits actually had a serious purpose. They drew attention to a war that could have gone almost unnoticed, with scant help for the United States' small, almost amateur navy. Jones's best weapon was his ability to panic the enemy, keep it off guard, and arrive where and when he was least expected.

Jones's affectionate side was not evident at sea. He was intelligent, charming, and courteous in social situations. He never married, but he loved his family. Jones never lacked for female companionship, and he regaled his audiences with tales of adventure at sea.

Jones held a special place in his heart for America's prisoners of war. These men waited months, sometimes years, to be part of a prisoner exchange. Great Britain treated captives harshly, sending them to prison ships or hard labor, regarding them as pirates. Many former

Prescribed Reading for Naval Academy Midshipmen

"None other than a Gentleman, as well as a Seaman, both in theory and in practice is qualified to support the character of a Commissioned Officer in the Navy, nor is any man fit to command a Ship of War who is not also capable of communicating his Ideas on Paper in Language that becomes his Rank."

—John Paul Jones to the Marine Committee, January 21, 1777[8]

prisoners joined *Bonhomme Richard*'s crew in gratitude for Jones's efforts on their behalf.

In December 1787, Jones wrote "If the new Constitution is adopted, as there is reason to expect, America will soon be a very respectable Nation; and the creation of a Marine Force will necessarily be among the first objects of her policy."[9] He lived to see the Constitution ratified in 1788, but he died before Congress created a new navy on March 27, 1794. It took the place of the navy of the American Revolution, which disbanded after the war. The new navy was formed in response to threats from the effects of the French Revolution and the Barbary pirates.

The modern-day United States Navy is fortunate to have had this insightful, complex, demanding, over-confident taskmaster in its perilous early years. He was in the right place in history at the right time. The United States will be forever in his debt.

CHRONOLOGY

1747—Born in Kirkcudbrightshire, Scotland, on July 6.

1761 –1768—Learns seamanship on *Friendship*, *King George*, and *Two Friends*.

1768—Takes command of *John* after the captain dies at sea; Crewman Mungo Maxwell dies at sea while Jones is captain of *John*; Becomes a Mason in Kirkcudbright.

1773—As captain of *Betsy*, kills mutinous sailor in self-defense.

1774—Begins a new life in America.

1775—First lieutenant aboard Continental Navy's *Alfred*.

1775 –1776—Captain of *Providence*.

1776—Captain of *Alfred*.

1777 –1778—Captain of *Ranger*; Defeats H.M.S. *Drake* in Ireland; American flag saluted by French fleet in Quiberon Bay; Whitehaven harbor, Selkirk mansion raids.

1779—Captain of *Bonhomme Richard*; Defeats H.M.S. *Serapis*; Captain of *Alliance*; Takes refuge in the Texel in Holland.

1780—Captain of *Ariel*.

1781—Captain of *America*; Congress gives *America* to France in appreciation for its help during the Revolutionary War; Receives French and American honors for bravery and military conduct.

1783 –1788—Revolutionary War ends; Jones pursues prize money in Europe.

1786—Presents *Memoire* (1775–1784) as a gift for King Louis XVI of France.

1788 –1789—Rear Admiral in Imperial Russian Navy.

1792—Dies July 18 in Paris, France.

1905—Jones's coffin found and his body identified; Jones's body returns to America escorted by eleven United States Navy ships.

1913—Placed in the chapel, United States Naval Academy, Annapolis, Maryland.

CHAPTER NOTES

Chapter 1. The Summer Cruise

1. William M. Fowler, Jr., *Rebels Under Sail* (New York: Charles Scribner's Sons, 1976), p. 167.

2. Nowland Van Powell, *The American Navies of the Revolutionary War* (New York: G.P. Putnam's Sons, 1974), p. 76.

3. Ibid.

Chapter 2. Going to Sea

1. Alan Villiers, *Men, Ships and the Sea* (Washington, D.C.: The National Geographic Society, 1973), p. 184.

2. Samuel Eliot Morison, *John Paul Jones: A Sailor's Biography* (Boston: Little, Brown and Company, 1959), p. 15.

3. Ibid., p. 20.

4. Ibid., p. 23.

Chapter 3. The Continental Navy

1. Barbara W. Tuchman, *The First Salute* (New York: Ballantine Books, 1988), p. 45.

2. Nowland Van Powell, *The American Navies of the Revolutionary War* (New York: G.P. Putnam's Sons, 1974), p. 30.

3. Tuchman, p. 48.

4. Ibid., p. 28.

5. Samuel Eliot Morison, *John Paul Jones: A Sailor's Biography* (Boston: Little, Brown and Company, 1959), p. 44.

6. Tuchman, p. 49.

7. Morison, p. 52.

Chapter 4. *Providence*

1. Samuel Eliot Morison, *John Paul Jones: A Sailor's Biography* (Boston: Little, Brown and Company, 1959), p. 60.

2. Ibid., p. 67.

3. Ibid., p. 93.

4. "Evolution of the United States Flag," *The United States Flag Page*, n.d., <http://www.usflag.org/flag.evolution.html> (November 16, 2000).

5. William M. Fowler, Jr., *Rebels Under Sail* (New York: Charles Scribner's Sons, 1976), p. 95.

Chapter 5. *Ranger*

1. Joseph G. Sawtelle, ed., *John Paul Jones and the Ranger* (Portsmouth, N.H.: Peter E. Randall Publisher, 1994), p. 1.

2. Ibid., p. 3.

3. Ibid., p. 5.

4. Ibid., p. 7.

5. William M. Fowler, Jr., *Rebels Under Sail* (New York: Charles Scribner's Sons, 1976), p. 95.

6. Samuel Eliot Morison, *John Paul Jones: A Sailor's Biography* (Boston: Little, Brown and Company, 1959), p. 135.

7. Ibid., pp. 134–135.

8. Sawtelle, p. 161.

9. Ibid., p. 162.

Chapter 6. Pirate or Patriot?

1. Joseph G. Sawtelle, ed., *John Paul Jones and the Ranger* (Portsmouth, N.H.: Peter E. Randall Publisher, 1994), p. 164.

2. Samuel Eliot Morison, *John Paul Jones: A Sailor's Biography* (Boston: Little, Brown and Company, 1959), p. 158.

3. Ibid., p. 159.

4. Ibid., p. 152.

5. Sawtelle, pp. 176–178.

6. Ibid., p. 180.

7. Ibid., pp. 181–183.

8. Ibid., pp. 184–185.

9. William M. Fowler, Jr., *Rebels Under Sail* (New York: Charles Scribner's Sons, 1976), p. 158.

Chapter 7. *Bonhomme Richard*

1. Samuel Eliot Morison, *John Paul Jones: A Sailor's Biography* (Boston: Little, Brown and Company, 1959), p. 205.

2. William M. Fowler, Jr., *Rebels Under Sail* (New York: Charles Scribner's Sons, 1976), p. 159.

3. Barbara W. Tuchman, *The First Salute* (New York: Ballantine Books, 1988), p. 46.

4. Nowland Van Powell, *The American Navies of the Revolutionary War* (New York: G.P. Putnam's Sons, 1974), p. 74.

5. Richard M. Ketchum, ed., *American Heritage History of the American Revolution* (New York: Bonanza Books, 1971), p. 278.

6. Fowler, p. 163.

7. Tuchman, p. 82.

8. Fowler, p. 147.

9. Van Powell, p. 76.

10. "Report of John Paul Jones, Cruise of U.S. Ship *Bonhomme Richard* and Squadron, and Capture of H.B.M. Ships *Serapis* and *Countess of Scarborough*," p. 13, <http://www.Seacoastnh.com> (August 23, 2001).

11. Tuchman, p. 83.

12. "Report of John Paul Jones," p. 15, <http://www.Seacoastnh.com> (August 23, 2001).

13. Morison, p. 236.

Chapter 8. The Texel and Beyond

1. Samuel Eliot Morison, *John Paul Jones: A Sailor's Biography* (Boston: Little, Brown and Company, 1959), p. 214.

2. Ibid., p. 246.

3. Richard M. Ketchum, ed., *The American Heritage History of the American Revolution* (New York: Bonanza Books, 1971), p. 274.

4. Barbara W. Tuchman, *The First Salute* (New York: Ballantine Books, 1988), p. 84.

5. Clara Ann Simmons, *John Paul Jones, America's Sailor* (Annapolis, Md.: Naval Institute Press), p. 67.

6. Morison, p. 265.

7. Ibid., p. 273.

8. Ibid., p. 250.

9. Ibid., pp. 294–295.

10. Ibid., p. 304.

Chapter 9. After the Revolution

1. Samuel Eliot Morison, *John Paul Jones: A Sailor's Biography* (Boston: Little, Brown and Company, 1959), p. 310.

2. Ibid., p. 279.

3. Ibid., p. 313.

4. Ibid.

5. Ibid., p. 317.

6. Ibid., p. 335.

7. Ibid., p. 340.

8. Ibid., p. 400.

Chapter 10. Epilogue

1. Samuel Eliot Morison, *John Paul Jones: A Sailor's Biography* (Boston: Little, Brown and Company, 1959), p. 402.

2. William M. Fowler, Jr., *Rebels Under Sail* (New York: Charles Scribner's Sons, 1976), p. 152.

3. Morison, p. 402.

4. "The Two Burials of John Paul Jones," <http://www.Seacoastnh.com/jpj/corpse2.html> (August 23, 2001).

5. Ibid.

6. "250th Anniversary of the Birth of John Paul Jones," *Department of the Navy-Naval Historical Center*, July 3, 1997, <http://www.history.navy.mil/faqs/faq58-1.htm> (February 2, 2000).

7. Barbara W. Tuchman, *The First Salute* (New York: Ballantine Books, 1988), p. 45.

8. "250th Anniversary of the Birth of John Paul Jones," *Department of the Navy-Naval Historical Center*, July 3, 1997, <http://www.history.navy.mil/faqs/faq58-1.htm> (February 2, 2000).

9. Dean Calbreath, "On the Way to the Millennium," *San Diego Union-Tribune*, October 13, 1999, p. A-2.

GLOSSARY

ballast—Heavy material, often rocks, carried in the bottom of a ship to give temporary or permanent stability.

blanketing—When one ship's sails cut off another ship's breeze, the blanketed sails cannot fill with wind to move the vessel forward.

bowsprit—A strong pole that projects from the front of a ship, often connected to a sail.

brigantine—Two-masted ship carrying a combination of square and triangular sails.

broadside—Firing all the guns on one side of a ship at once.

cannonballs—Round balls made from molten iron, in various weights to fit different sizes of cannons; a cannon was known by the weight of the ball it fired, as in a "twelve-pounder."

collier—Merchant ship equipped to transport coal.

come about—Nautical term for changing course and adjusting the sails to catch the wind from a new direction.

commodore—A courtesy title granted to the senior naval captain in command of a squadron or fleet; later became an official rank for a flag officer in the United States Navy.

fore and aft—At or toward the front and rear of a craft.

frigate—Fast nineteenth-century naval vessel with elaborate sails and cannons on one or two decks.

grapeshot—Cluster of small iron balls fired from a cannon.

guillotine—Device for beheading a person by dropping a wide blade on the back of the neck from a height.

H.M.S.—British Navy's abbreviation for "His or Her Majesty's Ship."

hull—The frame or body of a ship.

merchantman—Term for cargo ships used in commerce and trade.

press gang—Group of sailors, led by an officer, who enlisted other men into the service, sometimes by force; men were "impressed" off the streets, through raids, and out of jails during desperate times.

privateers—Privately owned ships that attack enemy ships in wartime for profit.

rake—Fire guns along the full length of a ship's hull, the partially submerged shell that supports the decks, and upper parts of the vessel.

rigging—The lines and chains on a ship that support the masts, sails, yards, and booms, allowing them to function properly.

sloop—Single-masted ship with sails that parallel a front-to-back, bow-to-stern, alignment; sloop-of-war had one deck of cannons.

states' navies—Eleven colonies formed fleets to protect their coastlines and harbors against British invaders; states' navies were little help to the Continental Navy and kept needed resources out of circulation. The Connecticut State Navy was the exception. It made trips to the West Indies for sulphur to make gunpowder.

FURTHER READING

Books

Dolan, Edward F. *The American Revolution: How We Fought the War of Independence.* Brookfield, Conn.: Millbrook Press, Incorporated, 1995.

Gilkerson, William. *The Ships of John Paul Jones.* Annapolis, Md.: Naval Institute Press, 1987.

Graff, Stewart. *John Paul Jones: Sailor Hero.* New York: Chelsea House Publishers, 1993.

January, Brendan. *The Revolutionary War.* Danbury, Conn.: Children's Press, 2000.

Lutz, Norma Jean. *John Paul Jones: Father of the U.S. Navy.* New York: Chelsea House Publishers, 1999.

Morison, Samuel Eliot. *John Paul Jones: A Sailor's Biography.* Boston: Little, Brown and Company, 1959.

Simmons, Clara Ann. *John Paul Jones, America's Sailor.* Annapolis, Md.: Naval Institute Press, 1997.

Smolinski, Diane. *Naval Warfare of the Revolutionary War.* Oxford: Heinemann Library, 2001.

Internet Addresses

"250th Anniversary of the Birth of John Paul Jones." *Department of the Navy: Naval Historical Center.* May 18, 2001. <http://www.history.navy.mil/faqs/faq58-1.htm>.

"John Paul Jones, 1747–92." *Maritime History and Naval Heritage Web Site.* n.d. <http://www.cronab.demon.co.uk/br11.htm>.

"John Paul Jones Articles and Resources." *SeacoastNH.com.* 1997–2001. <http://www.seacoastnh.com/jpj/index.html>.

"The War at Sea . . ." *The American Revolution Home Page.* 1998–1999. <http://webpages.homestead.com/revwar/files/sea.htm>.

INDEX